LINGUISTICS ACROSS CULTURES

linguistics
ACROSS
cultures

Applied Linguistics for Language Teachers

by ROBERT LADO
with a Foreword by Charles C. Fries

Ann Arbor — The University of Michigan Press

FOREWORD

The struggle to apply to the problems of foreign language learning the new views of language arising out of "structural" analyses has served to shift the focus of first attention from methods and techniques of teaching to the basis upon which to build these materials. The fundamental feature of the "new approach," therefore, is not a matter of a greater allotment of time, nor of smaller classes, nor even of greater emphasis on oral practice — desirable as these may be. Before any of the questions of how to teach a foreign language must come the much more important preliminary work of finding the special problems arising out of any effort to develop a new set of language habits against a background of different native language habits. A child in learning his native language has learned not only to attend to (receptively and productively) the particular contrasts that function as signals in that language; he has learned to *ignore* all those features that do not so function. He has developed a special set of "blind spots" that prevent him from responding to features that do not constitute the contrastive signals of his native language. Learning a second language, therefore, constitutes a very different task from learning the first language. The basic problems arise not out of any essential difficulty in the features of the new language themselves but primarily out of the special "set" created by the first language habits.

Robert Lado was the first to grasp the significance of these basic facts for the building of efficient valid measures of achievement and progress in mastering a foreign language. He has during the last ten years produced a variety of tests thus built upon a careful systematic comparison of the descriptive structural analyses of two languages — the native language of a group of students and the foreign language these students were striving to master. His comparisons demanded more and more complete descriptions, including not only the narrowly linguistic features but a wide selection of the social-cultural features in which the languages operated. He found similar "blind spots" throughout the whole range of linguistic-social-cultural features — "blind spots" that must be overcome if sound intercultural understanding was to be achieved — the fundamental objective of all language teaching.

This book, arising out of his long and fruitful experience, presents a practical approach to the kind of systematic linguistic-cultural comparisons that must form the basis of satisfactory teaching materials for the "new approach."

Charles C. Fries

This book is affectionately dedicated
TO MOTHER
Monolingual Spanish speaker in the U.S.A.

PREFACE

This book presents a fairly new field of applied linguistics and the analysis of culture, namely the comparison of any two languages and cultures to discover and describe the problems that the speakers of one of the languages will have in learning the other. The results of such comparisons have proved of fundamental value for the preparation of teaching materials, tests, and language learning experiments. Foreign language teachers who understand this field will acquire insights and tools for evaluating the language and culture content of textbooks and tests, supplementing the materials in use, preparing new materials and tests, and diagnosing student difficulties accurately.

The plan of the book rests on the assumption that we can predict and describe the patterns that will cause difficulty in learning, and those that will not cause difficulty, by comparing systematically the language and culture to be learned with the native language and culture of the student. In our view, the preparation of up-to-date pedagogical and experimental materials must be based on this kind of comparison. It has been our experience, further, that able foreign language teachers with proper guidance can carry out such comparisons with satisfactory precision, and I assume that psychologists who know a foreign language well can do likewise.

The style of presentation is addressed primarily to the trained teacher of foreign languages. It is hoped that with proper incentive and favorable circumstances he may apply the material to the preparation of better textbooks, tests, articles, and experiments, and contribute to the general improvement of the teaching and testing of foreign languages. If he is not a trained linguist he will not be able to apply the knowledge gained from these discussions to any and all languages, but he should be able to apply it to his native language and the foreign language he teaches. The style is addressed also to psychologists and educational psychologists interested in research on foreign language learning.

The trained linguist should not be misled by the effort of the author to achieve a nontechnical style. The statements and suggestions contained in these chapters can be translated into rigorous formulas that would satisfy him. Some of the linguistic observations presented here have not been previously reported in print anywhere.

This book was begun as part of a larger volume on language and culture testing, yet to be completed. As the writing progressed it became apparent that the discussions of techniques for comparison of languages and cultures had significance for teaching and research as well as for testing. It was therefore decided to release this material as a separate publication before those parts dealing exclusively with testing could be finished.

A great deal of what is brought together here appeared in separate articles in *Language Learning, The Modern Language Journal,* and *Hispania.* Comments by readers and additional experience gained by the author have permitted a more complete understanding of the comparison of languages and cultures.

Robert Lado

Ann Arbor, Michigan

CONTENTS

Chapter 1

THE NECESSITY FOR A SYSTEMATIC COMPARISON
OF LANGUAGES AND CULTURES

1. Introduction: Fundamental Assumption.

1.1 The fundamental assumption guiding the preparation of teaching materials at the English Language Institute of the University of Michigan is given by Fries: "The most effective materials are those that are based upon a scientific description of the language to be learned, carefully compared with a parallel description of the native language of the learner."[1]
Comparisons of English and several other languages were also made in preparation for the English textbooks of the A.C.L.S.,[2] and various articles dealing with partial comparisons of languages appear in the journal *Language Learning* as a contribution to foreign language learning research.[3]

1.2 The same assumption, that in the comparison between native and foreign language lies the key to ease or difficulty in foreign language learning, was applied to the preparation of language achievement tests by Lado.[4]

1.3 A practical confirmation of the validity of our assumption has come from the work of linguists who study the effect of close contact between languages in bilingual situations. They report that many linguistic distortions heard among bilinguals correspond to describable differences in the languages involved. Extensive studies have been carried out by Haugen and Weinreich in this area.[5]

1.4 Research in the psychology of language and in language

---

[1]Charles C. Fries, *Teaching and Learning English as a Foreign Language* (Ann Arbor: Univ. Mich. Press, 1945), p. 9.

[2]*Spoken English Textbooks*, ed. Martin Joos, American Council of Learned Societies. Program in English as a Foreign Language (Washington, D. C., 1954).

[3]*Language Learning*. A Journal of Applied Linguistics (Ann Arbor: Research Club in Language Learning). See Index to Vols. 1 through 5 in 5, No. 3-4 (1955).

[4]Robert Lado, "Measurement in English as a Foreign Language, with Special Reference to Spanish-Speaking Adults" (Doctoral dissertation, University of Michigan, 1951). See also articles by Lado in *Language Learning* and *The Modern Language Journal*.

[5]Einar Haugen, *The Norwegian Language in America* (Philadelphia: Univ. Penn. Press, 1953). Uriel Weinreich, *Languages in Contact* (New York: Publications of the Linguistic Circle of New York, 1953).

learning in educational psychology has not as a rule made any
conscious systematic use of assumptions of importance of the
native language habits in foreign language learning. Yet there is
every reason to believe that real progress could be made if such
assumptions were to become part of the planning in language
learning research.

1.5 Implied in Fries' assumption for effective teaching materials, and as observed in bilingual studies and in testing research,
is the fundamental assumption of this book: that individuals tend
to transfer the forms and meanings, and the distribution of forms
and meanings of their native language and culture to the foreign
language and culture — both productively when attempting to speak
the language and to act in the culture, and receptively when attempting to grasp and understand the language and the culture as
practiced by natives.

2. Significance for Teaching.

2.1 The teacher of foreign languages may wonder why he has
to go through the painful business of comparing languages. Is it
not his responsibility simply to teach a foreign language? Is it
not enough that he should know that foreign language?

Not if our assumption is correct. We assume that the student
who comes in contact with a foreign language will find some features of it quite easy and others extremely difficult. Those elements that are similar to his native language will be simple for
him, and those elements that are different will be difficult. The
teacher who has made a comparison of the foreign language with
the native language of the students will know better what the real
learning problems are and can better provide for teaching them.
He gains an insight into the linguistic problems involved that cannot easily be achieved otherwise.

In practice a teacher may be called upon to apply this knowledge under various circumstances. He may be asked to evaluate
materials before they are adopted for use. He may be asked to
prepare new materials. He may have to supplement the textbook
assigned to his class. And he will at all times need to diagnose
accurately the difficulties his pupils have in learning each pattern.

2.2 *Evaluating the language and culture content of a textbook*.
On the surface, most textbooks look pretty much alike. Publishers
see to it that their books look attractive and that the titles sound
enticing. That is part of their business. If a teacher is professionally trained, however, he will be able to look beyond attractive
illustrations and handsome printing and binding.

He should be able to see whether the book presents the language and culture patterns that form the system to be studied, and does not merely list disparate items from here and there. He should also be able to discern whether the book gives due emphasis to those patterns that are difficult because they are different from those of the native language of the students.

Some books, advertised as panaceas for easy learning of a foreign language, simply present a few patterns that are similar to the native language and spend a good many chapters, sometimes an entire volume, on them. The untrained teacher and student may get the impression that the book does simplify the learning of the language. But in reality it does not teach the foreign language; it merely entertains teacher and student in easy but unproductive activity. That weakness is immediately laid bare by comparing the two languages.

Textbooks should be graded as to grammatical structure, pronunciation, vocabulary, and cultural content. And grading can be done best after the kind of comparison we are presenting here.

2.3 *Preparing new teaching materials.* More and more the teacher is faced with the need to prepare textbooks and other teaching materials that are up to date and meet the needs of the particular students he is interested in. The most important new thing in the preparation of teaching materials is the comparison of native and foreign language and culture in order to find the hurdles that really have to be surmounted in the teaching. It will soon be considered quite out of date to begin writing a textbook without having previously compared the two systems involved.

Other advances in techniques of presentation of language and culture should not be neglected, but the linguistic comparison is basic and really inescapable if we wish to make progress and not merely reshuffle the same old materials.

2.4 *Supplementing inadequate materials.* Commonly, the teacher finds that he is given an assigned textbook that he finds inadequate both as to linguistic and cultural content. The teacher who has systematically compared the two languages will be able to prepare supplementary exercises on those patterns which are important or difficult and have been overlooked or treated inadequately in the book.

2.5 *Diagnosing difficulties.* The teacher will at all times in working with his students be faced with the need to diagnose quickly and accurately the problems troubling a student. Much misinformation and many misleading explanations can be and are given students in the attempt to help them. Knowing not only what the pattern is, but knowing precisely what feature in that pattern is troubling the student and what different feature he is substituting can lead to a simple hint or pointer that may solve an otherwise baffling situation. The professionally trained teacher should notice not only a "foreign" accent or an "incorrect" form but a clear-cut, specific distortion of a sound, construction, or cultural pattern.

3. Significance for Testing.

3.1 A major advance has already been achieved in tests of English as a foreign language, largely as a result of the linguistic comparison of English and the native language of the student. With the results of such a comparison we know pretty accurately just what the learning problems are, and we can concentrate our ingenuity on how to test them. It so happens that language problems are very stable and specific, and we can observe our results rather well.

Language testing in the past had tended either toward rules and lists of words or, as a reaction against that extreme, toward another extreme: reading of connected passages, writing a composition, conversing, or listening to connected materials, without regard to their language content. The testing of rules and lists of words did not have many wholehearted friends, in the United States at least. It was already out of fashion, and rightly so, if for no other reason than because knowledge of rules and memorization of lists of words seemed to bear no relation to being able to speak the language and understand it or even to read it.

The reaction against rules and lists of words turned to what seemed like a "common sense" solution: the use of connected materials. The failure in the use of these lay in disregarding their language content. The number of passages and compositions that could be expressed in language are infinite, and it is easy to find a passage or a composition topic in which one might do badly even knowing the language. How well would the average reader do if asked to write a five-hundred-word composition explaining the theory of relativity even in his native language? How well would he understand a professional lecture on that topic in that same language?

The advance in English language testing came not from connected material but from concentrating on the language problems as they actually are. And we get closest to the language problems by a systematic comparison of the native language and the foreign language. The alternative attempt, to find valid problems by the statistical treatment of connected material which is not chosen linguistically, does not seem productive. It will tend to leave out problems that are important. It will tend to include problems which are not properly language. And it involves elaborate tabulation of large amounts of materials that could be avoided. Statistical treatment has its place in the refinement of the test, not in the selection of language problems.

The application of linguistic comparison to testing seems a most promising field. There is little doubt that the results will be rewarding. The application of the techniques of linguistic comparison to cultural comparison is now being explored and has already shown positive results for testing of cultural understanding.

3.2 *Progress in testing pronunciation.* Nowhere is there a more dramatic case of progress in language testing than the one which is taking place in testing pronunciation. In less than five years the testing of pronunciation in English as a foreign language changed from the realm of intangibles to become the easiest, most accessible area of language testing. And this change is directly connected to the application of phonemic linguistic comparison to the selection of the problems to be tested.

We used to talk in vague terms about foreign accent, comprehensibility, amusing errors in pronunciation, and the like, or we avoided the problem of testing pronunciation altogether. We can now test the entire sound system of a language in a test of reasonable size, and we can score the test objectively. We can test the student's perception of the significant sound contrasts of the language through his comprehension of carefully chosen sentences. We can test that perception by asking him if two sentences he hears are the same or different. We can test his production of the significant sounds by forcing him to utter carefully chosen sentences. And we can test his pronunciation indirectly by asking him to say whether certain sounds whose symbols are omitted in a printed test are the same or different to him.

These techniques for testing pronunciation may seem the real contribution, but the fact of the matter is that they could not have been devised if we did not know quite specifically what problems we were trying to test. And even if the techniques alone had been devised, they would remain pretty ineffective unless we were able to sharpen them to get at the pronunciation problems of our students.

3.3 *On grammatical structure.* Had the study of grammar remained a matter of memorizing rules of artificial correctness, or had it remained a matter of arguing over this or that expression as correct or incorrect, there would not be any point in comparing two grammatical structures for testing purposes. Grammar as grammatical structure — as patterned elements of speech that convey meanings in a language — permits a new view of the testing of grammar. We do not test the student on the correctness of this or that phrase. We test him on his comprehension of the grammatical meaning of the sentence, or we test his ability to express a grammatical meaning through the patterns of the foreign language.

The view of grammar as grammatical structure opens the way to a comparison of the grammatical structure of the foreign language with that of the native language to discover the problems of the student in learning the foreign language. The results of such a comparison tell us what we should test and what we should not test, it helps us devise test items and techniques that also look quite acceptable from a common-sense point of view, and — this is the important consideration — we can actually test the control of the language on the part of the student. We have already devised techniques involving sentence comprehension, continuing a conversation, and reconstructing incomplete sentences that actually bring out specific problems in mastering the grammatical structure of English.

3.4 *On vocabulary testing.* The vocabulary of a language is inadequately represented by any list, even if it is a frequency list. Some words are used primarily for grammatical functions, others are used as substitutes for other words, and all have various meanings and uses. Because of the large number of words in any language, we have to select a sample for testing; we cannot use all of them. And a sample will not be valid unless the various kinds of words are adequately represented.

Now, the moment you select a random vocabulary sample in a foreign language you immediately discover that some words will be easy because they resemble native-language words, while others will present various kinds of difficulties because they differ from the native language in various ways. We can, therefore, make a further selection of the vocabulary to be used in a test by comparing it with the native-language vocabulary of the students. The result will be a more compact, more effective test through selection of words that are representative of the vocabulary difficulties that our student will find and through selection of those features of meaning that will be most revealing.

3.5 *Cultural understanding.* The idea that we might be able to test the understanding of a foreign culture objectively seems impossible to most people today. We know so little about the structure of our own culture, let alone that of a foreign one. And how can you compare cultures anyway?

Even though this is virtually a virgin field, we have already been able to describe specific patterns of behavior in a given culture and through comparison with the native culture of the student we have discovered that there are certain misunderstandings that take place again and again. Good experimental test items have been worked out from the information yielded by that partial comparison of cultural behavior, and we have every reason to believe that much more complete testing of cultural understanding can be carried out with present tools.

4. Significance for Research.

The same error that held back progress in language testing — that is, the assumption that any sample of a language represents the learning problems for that language — is holding back progress in research on the psychology of language learning. Not knowing what the learning problems are, experimenters adhere only to the externals of experimental design, and their results are either invalid or meaningless. How can we design a meaningful experiment on the effectiveness of an oral technique if we do not know specifically what the student is to learn, and what he already knows because it is the same as in his native language? Major experiments in recent years have proved inconclusive because the experimenters made no distinction between those elements of the language that really had to be learned and those that did not. Simply speaking some sentences and checking comprehension does not ensure coverage of what the student has to learn, and certainly two sentences are not linguistically the same simply because they rank the same in difficulty.

Lacking specific understanding of the language problems that merit research, some psychologists have taken refuge in mass experimentation. If we use hundreds or thousands of subjects we average out any inequalities in our data, they argue. The sad result may be that they also average out the very differences that would give the information desired. And since mass experiments are not possible without major financial support, the great possibilities of individual research are discouraged or even lost.

By using the results of linguistic and cultural comparison of the native and the foreign languages and cultures, we can pinpoint our research problems, and individuals can carry out highly significant and sorely needed experiments singlehanded.

5. Significance for General Understanding.

A good-hearted person, anxious to help toward the unification of mankind, wondered if this business of comparing languages and cultures did not tend to divide. Was it not better to ignore the differences, she thought. Were we not all the same fundamentally?

Certainly I believe that we are all one flock, that we are the same fundamentally. But because human personality has evolved a variety of ways to live, ways that we call cultures, we constantly misinterpret each other across cultures. If we ignore these cultural differences we will misjudge our cultural neighbors — as we constantly do at present — for a form of behavior that to them has one meaning may have another one to us. And if we do not know of the difference in meaning we will ascribe to our neighbors the intentions that the same behavior would imply for us, and would pass on them the same judgment as on our confreres. In fact, I am afraid that we do exactly that in most cases at present.

If, on the other hand, we know that an item of behavior has a different meaning in the other culture we will not misunderstand. And we will have a chance to understand ourselves and what we do much better as a result. We will be able to establish genuine habits of tolerance, rather than naive good intentions that crumble the first time our cultural neighbor does something which is perfectly all right in his culture but strange or misleading in ours. In visiting a foreign country we will actually be able to enter into its life and understand and be understood.

Again, in the realm of language rather than that of culture as such, the harm that we do our students by not teaching them a foreign language or by teaching it as if it were just different words from those of our own language lies in the false idea they will hold of what it means to learn a foreign language. They will never be ready to struggle to pronounce things in different sound units, different intonation, different rhythm and stress, different constructions, and even different units of meaning unless they realize that this is exactly what's involved in learning a foreign language, and that although learning those things will require effort, often dull and uninteresting, the rewards for the effort will be great.

We have explored some of the many contributions that systematic comparison of native and foreign language and culture can make to education and research. The following chapters present working techniques to carry out specific comparisons of two systems of pronunciation, grammatical structure, vocabulary, writing, and cultural behavior.

Chapter 2

HOW TO COMPARE TWO SOUND SYSTEMS

1. Introduction.

1.1 *The phoneme.* It is important to keep in mind that the sounds of human language are more than just sound. The *p* of *pin* is exploded with a puff of air following it, whereas the *p* of *capture* is not. Those two sounds are quite different as mere sound. But in English we say they are the "same," and they are, because they function as the same unit in the sound system of English. These functioning units like English /p/ are called *phonemes* by structural linguists and usually will be enclosed in slant bars in the text. *establish the phonemes of each lang.*

1.2 *Phonemes are not letters.* Sometimes a letter of the alphabet may represent a phoneme, as the *p* in *pin* and *capture,* but a phoneme is never a letter; it is a unit of sound. Chinese does not have letters, yet it has phonemes. And even the letter *p* does not always represent the phoneme /p/ in English. Take for example the letter *p* in *telephone.* It certainly does not represent the phoneme /p/ there. Phonemes are units of sound that exist in all the languages we know, whether or not they have ever been written.

1.3 *Phonemic versus non-phonemic differences.* Is it not a paradox that two sounds which are different as sound, for example the *p*'s in *pin* and *capture,* are considered the "same" phoneme? It may seem so, but it is quite easy to understand if we realize that there are two kinds of differences in the sounds of a language. One kind is represented by the difference between the exploded, aspirated *p* of *pin* and the unexploded *p* of *capture.* This difference is never used in English to distinguish any two words. Even if we artificially pronounce *capture* with the *p* of *pin,* it will remain the same word. We will call that kind of difference *non-phonemic* or non-significant. The other kind of difference is represented by the phonemes /p/ and /b/ in *pin* and *bin* for example. This difference is constantly used in English to distinguish words. We call it a *phonemic* difference. All languages have hundreds or even thousands of non-phonemic differences. On the other hand, any one language has a relatively small number of phonemic distinctions.

9

The clear understanding of phonemic differences is the contribution of modern structural linguistics. This level of analysis, the phonemic level, is the "new" thing in the study of the sound systems of languages.

1.4 *A sound system.* A phoneme is a complex unit in the system of a language. The English phoneme /p/, for example, contrasts minimally with /b/ in the pair *roping* and *robing* and many others. In that particular pair, the voicing of /b/ is the dominant feature of difference — in /b/ the vocal chords continue to vibrate to produce voicing, while in /p/ they are silent for a split second. The same phoneme /p/ contrasts minimally with /f/ not by voicing but principally by manner of articulation in the pair *dipper: differ.* A difference in point of articulation accompanies the contrast but does not decide it. The same phoneme /p/ contrasts minimally with /t/ not by voicing or manner of articulation but by point of articulation. Other contrasts such as /p/ and /m/, /p/ and /k/ depend on still other features of articulation. The point is that English /p/ is part of a system of contrasts which are peculiar to English and which operate now in one direction, now in another. We would really need a many-dimensional model to represent all these interacting contrasts. The phonemic field of English /p/ might be partly represented by a figure such as the one that follows.

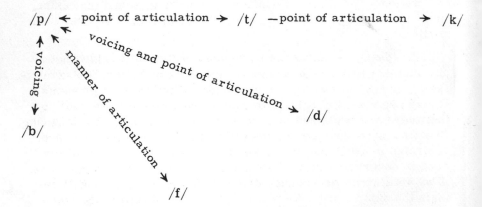

1.5 *A system of habits.* The amazing thing is that a normal speaker of a language uses this complex system of contrasts with great speed and the greatest of ease. He is not even aware in most instances that he is using such a system. This feat can be accomplished by reducing most of the operation of the system to automatic or semi-automatic habits.

1.6 *Great strength of the system*. Probably because the use of the sound system of a language operates as a system of automatic and semi-automatic habits, it is extremely difficult to change anything in that system. There is an unbelievably strong force binding the units — the phonemes — of any language in their complex of contrasts. The adult speaker of one language cannot easily pronounce language sounds of another even though he has no speech impediment, and what is even more startling, he cannot easily hear language sounds other than those of his native language even though he suffers no hearing defect.

1.7 *Transfer of native sound system*. We have ample evidence that when learning a foreign language we tend to transfer our entire native language system in the process. We tend to transfer to that language our phonemes and their variants, our stress and rhythm patterns, our transitions, our intonation patterns and their interaction with other phonemes.

Production distortions. Thus we can understand the widely observed fact that the pronunciation of a German speaker learning English is quite noticeably different from that of a Spanish speaker learning English, and both are quite different from that of a Chinese speaker learning the same variety of English. And we understand further that the distortions in the English pronunciation of a German speaker will bear great similarity to the distortions of other German speakers, just as the distortions in the English pronunciation of a Spanish or Chinese speaker are similar to those of other speakers of the same language.

Perception blind spots. Much less known, and often not even suspected, may be the fact mentioned above that the speaker of one language listening to another does not actually hear the foreign language sound units — phonemes. He hears his own. Phonemic differences in the foreign language will be consistently missed by him if there is no similar phonemic difference in his native language. The Thai language makes a phonemic distinction between aspirated and unaspirated *p*. In English that difference is not phonemic, and as a result English speakers learning Thai usually do not hear the difference between the two *p* sounds in Thai.

1.8 *Comparison of sound systems*. We now see more clearly the need for comparing the native and the foreign sound systems as a means of predicting and describing the pronunciation problems of the speakers of a given language learning another.

Since the transfer is usually in one direction, from the native language to the foreign language, an analysis with English as the

foreign language is not the same as one with English as the native
language.

1.9 *Applications*. Even though the process of comparing two
sound systems must of necessity be tedious, dry, and abstract, the
results obtained are of great practical use for the preparation of
textbooks, tests, and exercises to supplement inadequate materials, and for the evaluation of materials and the diagnosis of student problems.

And again, even though the work described in the remainder of
this chapter may be dry and occasionally difficult, the results
when used in actual lesson materials may be made as interesting
and challenging as the creativeness of the textbook writer or
teacher can make them.   •

2. Problem Analysis: Sound Segments.

2.1 In learning the sound system of a foreign language one
finds sounds that are physically similar to those of the native
language, that structure similarly to them, and that are similarly distributed. "Learning" of such phonemes occurs by simple
transfer without difficulty. On the other hand, one also finds
sounds that are not part of the sound system of the native language, that structure differently, or that are differently distributed. Learning of these occurs more slowly, and difficulty with
them is more persistent. In fact, learning of the latter actually
means learning the sounds of the language. We therefore seek to
find those problems, and we will find them by the structural comparison of the two sound systems.

Such a comparison, if it is to be complete and accurate, involves linguistic manipulations which are not usually described
in the literature. I found it helpful to follow certain procedures
in handling data which should prove helpful to others. These
procedures, however, are not intended as a rigid step-by-step
approach but as a simple summing up of the important things involved in such work. They are presented here in three stages:
linguistic analysis of sound systems, comparison of sound systems, and description of troublesome contrasts.

2.2 *Analysis of sound systems*. The object here is to find or
prepare a linguistic analysis of the sound system of the language
to be learned and a similar description of the language of the
learner. It is crucial to find good descriptions. As a rule we
will not be able to use the descriptions found in ordinary textbooks since, except for those few which have made deliberate use

of scientific linguistic data, the descriptions will not be complete
or will be inaccurately stated. The descriptions should include
segmental phonemes and phonemes of stress, intonation, and
juncture or transition. They should include relevant data on the
phonetic features of the phonemes and their variants and on their
distribution. These data constitute what is generally called the
phonology of a language.

2.3 *Comparison of units.* In comparing the sound systems of a
foreign language and the native language I find it good safe practice to take up each phoneme separately regardless of any general
patterns of difference I may have observed. The comparison of
each phoneme should include at least three checks: (1) Does the
native language have a phonetically similar phoneme? (2) Are
the variants of the phonemes similar in both languages? (3) Are
the phonemes and their variants similarly distributed? Let's
take up each of these queries separately with segmental phonemes
first. Later we will apply the same approach to the phonemes of
stress and of intonation.

2.4 *Location and description of segmental problems.* Does
the native language have a phonetically similar phoneme? Experience shows that when the foreign language uses a phoneme
which does not exist in the learner's native language, that is,
when there is no phoneme in the native language that could be
transferred to the foreign language and actually function as the
phoneme in question, the student will not be able to produce that
phoneme readily in learning the foreign language. He will substitute some other phoneme from his native stock. Experience
and experiments also show that the learner will have trouble
hearing as well as producing the new phoneme.

Let me illustrate. In comparing the sound system of English
with that of Portuguese, we would find that Portuguese does not
have phonemes that might pass as English /č ǰ θ ð h r y w / as in
chew, jump, ether, either, hose, rose, year, we're, respectively.
Portuguese speakers will have difficulty pronouncing and hearing
these phonemes. We would consider them pronunciation problems.

Similarly, if the comparison is between English and Spanish,
we find that Spanish does not have a number of phonemes that are
part of the sound system of English. Spanish does not have /v/
as in *vote,* /ð/ as in *then,* /z/ as in *zoo,* /ž/ as in *pleasure,* /š/
as in *shoe,* /ǰ/ as in *jump,* and several of the vowels. These phonemes will be difficult for Spanish speakers to pronounce and to

hear and will therefore constitute important pronunciation problems.[1]

We see that even in learning the same foreign language, English in this case, each linguistic background will have a different
set of phonemes representing problems for that group of speakers.

The first phase of comparison, the comparison of the phonemes
as units, can be achieved quickly if we have a phonemic chart for
each of the two languages, the native and the foreign. For con-
venience both charts should be based on the same criteria of
classification: points of articulation horizontally with front of
vocal apparatus to the left of the page; air stream variations
vertically, with complete interruption at the top of the page, de-
creasing to the bottom. This particular arrangement is a con-
vention adopted from the usual practice in diagramming the vocal
apparatus facing left.

The preliminary comparison of full phonemes, with or without
the aid of phonemic charts, does not give us the complete picture
of the pronunciation problems of the student. In fact, it gives a
very incomplete picture, since in most cases the problem will not
be the total absence of a phoneme in a given language but a problem involving variants of phonemes. We will therefore find it
necessary to proceed with the second check: *If the native language has a similar phoneme, is the phonetic shape of its variants
similar also?* If it is, the student will have little or no trouble
producing that entire phoneme, except for matters of distribution
taken up below. Notice that I say "produce." There may still be
difficulty in recognizing it in contrast with another phoneme if the
other one does not exist in the native language. That problem
will be discussed in stage three, below.

If, on the other hand, the phonemes which we tentatively accepted as "similar" have phonetically different variants, we may
have located another pronunciation problem.

Problem: In comparing English with Spanish, when first
checking English /d/ we might tentatively say that Spanish has a
similar phoneme /d/ and therefore not consider it a problem. At
the second query, "Are its variants also similar?" we would find
that Spanish /d/ has two well-defined variants, a stop variant [d]
as in *dos* 'two,' and a fricative variant [đ] as in *lado* 'side.' The
situation, then, is more complex than it seemed on first inspection. What we have is a Spanish stop variant [d] which "resembles" English /d/ as in *day*, and a Spanish fricative variant [đ]

[1]David W. Reed, Robert Lado, and Yào Shen, "The Importance of the Native Language
in Foreign Language Learning," *Language Learning*, 1, No. 1 (1948), 17-23.

which resembles English /ð/ as in *they,* two different phonemes
in the sound system of English, but only one phoneme in Spanish.

We know from experience that Spanish speakers will transfer
their entire /d/ phoneme into English and therefore automatically
produce the [đ] variant between vowels and after /r/, the environments in which it normally occurs in Spanish. Spanish speakers will thus say *lather* instead of *ladder, wreathing* instead of
reading, etc.

We conclude then that the English phoneme /d/, although not a
pronunciation problem as a total unit, is in fact a phonemic problem between vowels and after /r/ for Spanish speakers.

As a matter of fact, my experience on the basis of test evidence has been that the kind of problem in which part of a phoneme in the native language can pass as a separate phoneme in
the foreign language, and other parts of the same native-language
phoneme pass as a different phoneme in the foreign language —
that kind of problem is by far the most difficult one to overcome.
Difficulty in hearing the English contrast between /d/ and /ð/ is
by actual computation of test data one of the most stubborn hearing difficulties for Spanish speakers.

The above observation is not limited to pronunciation matters,
but applies to vocabulary and grammatical matters as well.
Stated in more general terms, when one significant unit or element in the native language equates bilingually with two significant units in the foreign language we have maximum learning
difficulty. In vocabulary, English *to be* corresponds to Spanish
ser and *estar,* and results in a major problem for English speakers learning Spanish. In grammar, one Spanish question pattern,
¿Quién vino? ¿Dónde vive? corresponds to two English question
patterns, *Who came?* and *Where do you live?* The second of
these two patterns constitutes a major hurdle for Spanish speakers learning English.

Returning to our main concern at this time, pronunciation, one
may wonder about the limits of the criterion of phonetic similarity
between sounds in two languages. When are two sounds to be considered similar? Admittedly there is no clear-cut line separating
similar from dissimilar, precisely because sounds that are different in one language may be heard as similar in another, and vice
versa. We are able, nevertheless, to use the criterion to advantage by dealing with features of sound which in a variety of
languages are found to be significant phonetic components of phonemes. Among these features are vibration of the vocal chords
versus nonvibration (voiced versus voiceless sounds), air stream
flowing through the mouth, nose, or both (oral, nasal, nasalized

sounds), various kinds of articulation (stops, fricatives, affricates, etc.), various points of articulation (bilabial, labio-dental, dental, alveolar, palatal, velar, etc.).[2] The phonemic analysis that we need should include such phonetic data. It should list the phonemes, the phonetic features of the phonemes, and the principal variants and their distribution.

In general we will be able to complete our comparison on the basis of these descriptions. Occasionally, however, we may encounter differences in the theoretical analysis that on further observation turn out to be of no importance. For example, the point of articulation of Spanish /d/ is the inside of the front teeth — the tongue tip makes a fairly wide contact with the back of the front teeth. The point of articulation of English /d/ is the alveolar ridge above and behind the front teeth. At an early stage in the comparison one might decide that this difference in articulation is such that Spanish /d/, even the stop variant, will not function as English /d/. Experience, however, shows that it does, and that this difference in point of articulation is heard as a matter of "accent," Spanish accent, that does not change any word in the language. A reanalysis of the difference shows that dental versus alveolar articulation is never used in English as the only contrastive difference between phonemes: alveolar fricatives /s/ and /z/ are grooved sibilants — the tongue tip forms a groove with the alveolar ridge rather than lying flat against it; English interdentals are fricatives, not sibilants. The contrast involves the type of articulation, not just the point of articulation. We understand then how the stop variant of Spanish /d/ can and does function as English /d/ when Spanish speakers transfer it to English.

The above observation can be handled by expanding the question on similarity of variants, or by adding the question, "If the variants are different in the two languages, will they result in a different structural interpretation for each language?" In the problem just discussed, the answer would be that English /d/ and the stop variant of Spanish /d/ are different, but their structural interpretation would be the same, that is, they would both be interpreted as the phoneme /d/.

Even when we do not find any problem as a result of the first two queries, we may discover a pronunciation problem when we apply the third check: *Is the phoneme similarly distributed?*

---

[2] For a fuller description of phonetics in connection with phonemic analysis see Kenneth L. Pike, *Phonemics* (Ann Arbor: Univ. Mich. Press, 1947), Chaps. 1 and 2. See also phonetics in Bernard Bloch and George L. Trager, *Outline of Linguistic Analysis* (Baltimore: Linguistic Society of America, 1942).

Again we know from experience that even when the native language has a similar phoneme and the variants are similar, if it does not occur in the same position as in the native language, the student will have trouble producing and hearing it in the position in which it does occur in the foreign language.

Problem: In comparing French with English we would find that French /ž/ as in *jamais* has a parallel English phoneme /ž/ as in *measure*. We would find that its variants would not cause any particular difficulty. But in asking the third question (Is the phoneme similarly distributed?) we would notice that in French it appears at the beginning of words and in English it does not. English speakers will transfer their /ž/ phoneme with its limitations into French and will thus have difficulty with learning the word initial /ž/ in that language.

2.5 *Sequences of sounds.* By following through on this matter of distribution of each phoneme we would eventually locate all the sequences of phonemes that might cause difficulty. However, it may be more economical to compare syllable structure and any other sequence or distributional unit that may be significant in the languages involved. Distribution patterns may correlate with syllables, morphemes, words, position of stress, etc.

Example: Final consonant clusters in English are troublesome to many non-English speakers. Word final /-rd/ is frequent in English but nonexistent in Spanish, for example. A Spanish speaker therefore tends to say *car* for *card, beer* for *beard, her* for *heard*, etc. If we list this problem under the phoneme /d/ we will clutter up our analysis unduly, for we would also have to list /-ld -nd -zd -rld -bd -gd -ǰd -vd / etc. It is more economical and accurate to analyze the matter as a sequence problem.

As a sequence problem we observe that English has a large number of consonant clusters preceding final pause or internal open juncture. We observe also that Spanish permits very few consonants and no clusters before final pause and before open juncture. The problem then is not limited to /-rd/. The student will hear and produce *card, cart, Carl, carp, cars* all as *car*.

2.6 *The analysis of sequence problems.* At first glance the simplest way to analyze sequence problems in pronunciation would seem to be listing sequences in the foreign language and checking to see if they occur in the native language. If they do occur in the native language, they will presumably not be problems as sequences; if they do not occur in the native language, they will constitute pronunciation problems. /θr/ as in *three* occurs in English but does not occur in Spanish, for example. We can assume that /θr/ will constitute a problem for Spanish speakers learning English.

Experience shows, however, that difficulty does not depend exclusively on the sequence itself but also on the position in which the sequence occurs. /sp/, /sk/, and /st/ occur in both English and Spanish. Yet in English they occur word-initially, while in Spanish they are always preceded by a vowel. Compare English *spy, school, student* and Spanish *espía, escuela, estudiante,* etc. Even though the sequences occur in Spanish, because they do not occur initially we can assume that Spanish speakers will have difficulty pronouncing them word-initially in English.

Further analysis reveals that in English /sp/, /sk/, and /st/ occur initially in a syllable, whereas in Spanish the /s/ belongs to one syllable and the /p/, /t/, or /k/ to another, thus: *es-pía, es-cuela, es-tudiante.* The problem may now be described as difficulty with syllable-initial clusters /sp/, /sk/, and /st/ because in the native language such syllable clusters do not occur.[3] This difficulty is easily confirmed by observing the speech of Spanish speakers learning English.

It is obvious that we must consider the distributional positions of sound clusters in order to analyze adequately the pronunciation problems involved in them. The distributional units which are relevant on the basis of experience with many languages are the utterance, the word, the morpheme, and the syllable. Other phenomena which may often add to or replace these distributional units are stress and juncture or transition. Some linguists have sought to simplify this type of analysis when describing single languages by recognizing only the utterance as a distributional unit and admitting only utterance initial, utterance medial, and utterance final positions in their description. This restriction is arbitrary and does not account for the facts of many languages. Compare for example the /sp/ pattern mentioned above. If the description states only that /sp/ occurs in utterance initial, utterance medial, and utterance final positions in English, whereas in Spanish it occurs only in utterance medial position, the conclusion that the Spanish speaker's difficulty would be in utterance initial and utterance final positions, and not in utterance medial, would turn out to be false. The Spanish speaker will have difficulty with that cluster whenever it occurs in the same syllable, even in utterance medial position.

In summary then, to locate and describe sequence problems, we compare the sequences and the positions in which they occur.

---

[3] If we define syllable transition as a phonemic entity in Spanish, symbolizing it with /-/, we might also say that the sequences /sp/, /sk/, /st/ do not occur in Spanish, since we would have /s-p/, /s-k/, and /s-t/ instead.

When the native language does not have a sequence, or when a sequence does not occur in a position in which it does occur in the foreign language, we will have located a problem.

When all the problems have been located and described it will be more economical and more meaningful in presentation if instead of simply listing the problems as items they are grouped and classified into patterns. Thus /sp/, /sk/, /st/ are not really separate problems but three special cases of one problem: /s/ + consonant (p t k f m n l) in close transition within the same syllable.

2.7 *Difficulty in pronouncing a phoneme versus difficulty in pronouncing a sequence.* When we find a sequence in which one of the phonemes of the foreign language is not to be found in the native language, we of course could simply list the matter as a sequence problem. But this would be an incomplete statement since we know that the phoneme itself will be a problem. Such a problem should be listed as a phoneme problem, and as a sequence one.

2.8 *Difficulty in pronouncing a word versus difficulty in pronouncing a phoneme or a phoneme sequence.* Sometimes a student mispronounces a word although he has mastered the phonemes and sequences involved. The very fact of the pronunciation difficulty being limited to that word indicates that the problem is not one of mastering the sound system but simply a matter of not knowing how to pronounce that word. Even if the word were of high frequency we would not be interested in it in a list of pronunciation problems. It is really a vocabulary problem. *word*

Problem: A student mispronounces the word *hiccough* omitting the final /p/ and substituting vowels other than /ɪ/ and /ə/. The problem is to find out if these mispronunciations are due to lack of control of the phonemes or lack of knowledge of this particular word. If he can pronounce the word *cup*, which includes medial /ə/ and final /p/, and other words involving those same sounds, and if he pronounces medial /ɪ/ as in *hip, hic, stick*, we conclude that it is not a matter of pronouncing these phonemes or these sequences but a matter of not knowing the word *hiccough*. In a teaching situation we would proceed to teach the word. In a list of pronunciation problems we simply leave it out.

2.9 *Problems of spelling pronunciation.* In languages with writing systems that in some way represent sounds, the student often mispronounces words because of influences from those writing systems. When both the foreign language and the native language use the same alphabet, the problem may be traceable to one of two possible causes. One possibility is that the same symbol might represent two different sounds in the two languages. In such a case the student tends to transfer the native language symbolization to the foreign language.

Problem: An English speaker studying Spanish will sometimes pronounce the family name *Jiménez* as /ǰímmɪz/. As far as the sound systems are concerned he should have no difficulty in pronouncing /himɛ́nɛθ(~s)/ as it would be pronounced in Spanish. But the initial letter *J* so often represents the sound /ǰ/ as in *Jim* in English that he transfers that representation to Spanish. He also tends to transfer the representation of the final letter *z*, which often represents the consonant sound /z/ as in *zoo* in English. The changes in the vowels follow English unstressed vowel patterns once the stress is shifted to the first syllable.

Problem: A slight variation of the same problem appears in the Spanish word *hijo* 'son,' usually pronounced /íxo/ or /ího/. English speakers sometimes pronounce it /háɪǰo/. The letter *h* represents no sound at all in Modern Spanish, but English speakers tend to give it the value it has in English. The letter *i* often represents the diphthong /aɪ/ in English, especially preceding a single consonant followed by *e* as in *five, time, file, dime,* etc. The letter *j* represents the sound /ǰ/, as already mentioned. We thus see that the seemingly arbitrary pronunciation of *hijo* as /háɪǰo/ resulted from transfer of the English spelling symbolization to Spanish.

The other possibility of spelling interference with pronunciation arises with inconsistencies in the spelling of the foreign language. The symbol which in one word represents one sound turns out to represent a different sound in another word. The student mispronounces the word by assuming that the symbol represents the same sound in both cases.

Problem: Any student learning English might pronounce the words *honest, hour, honor* with an initial /h/ sound, when of course there is no /h/ in their pronunciation. The student may have simply generalized on the basis of the many words in which an initial letter *h* does represent an initial sound /h/. The false extension might be summarized as follows: *h* = /h/ in *hat, house, have, hand, head, hot,* etc., therefore *h* = /h/ in *honest, hour, honor*.

Conclusion: These are not pronunciation problems; they are spelling problems. If they apply to just one word, or a couple of them, they may more effectively be considered vocabulary matters. If they apply to a large number of words they may be considered and described as a pattern of spelling mispronunciation and listed as such.

In languages such as Chinese, which do not use letters but morpheme or word symbols, the problems will arise at the morpheme level rather than at the phoneme level.

2.10 *Pronunciation problems with words that show similarity in two languages.* Since words that are similar in form in two languages show patterns of correspondences between the foreign language and the native one, the student's mispronunciations will often be predictable in terms of those patterns.

Problem: The Spanish words *pino, fino, vino, signo, benigno,* etc. are cognate with English *pine, fine, wine, sign, benign,* etc. The same letter, *i,* represents the sound /i/ in Spanish and the diphthong /aɪ/ in English. Spanish speakers may attempt to pronounce English *fine* as /finɛ/, *pine* as /pinɛ/, etc. Yet we know that the student is able to pronounce the diphthong /aɪ/ and a final nasal because he has them in Spanish. Spelling is obviously a factor in determining the kind of substitution that is made, but we note also that the problem is connected with a pattern of words and that the sounds of the pattern in Spanish are identified with the words and transferred to English.

2.11 *Perception of phonemic contrast through nonphonemic sound features.* It occurs sometimes that a phonemic contrast which does not exist as a contrast in the native language and which should be expected to constitute a major problem is actually not a problem in the perception of sounds. Perception of the contrast may take place through some accompanying feature which, although phonemic in the native language, in the foreign language is nonphonemic.

Problem: The contrast between English /i/ as in *beat* and /ɪ/ as in *bit* does not exist in German and would be expected to constitute a pronunciation problem both in speaking and in listening. Yet German speakers will identify the two sounds readily when those sounds are presented in minimal contrast. In most situations English /i/ is longer than /ɪ/, although this difference in length can be proved not to be a phonemic feature. The proof is very simple. One can speak the word *beat* quite short and the word *bit* quite long, and they will still remain two distinct words for English speakers. If length and not vowel quality were phonemic, the two words would have eventually been confused by native speakers. The quality of the two vowels is the deciding phonemic feature. The German speaker cannot hear clearly this difference in quality, but he hears a difference in length, because vowel length is phonemic in German. Final proof is obtained by deliberately shortening the /i/ and lengthening the /ɪ/. The German speaker then has difficulty keeping them separate while the English speaker is not bothered at all.

Conclusion: The contrast between /i/ and /ɪ/ need not be considered a perception problem. It is a speaking problem, since the German speaker will produce a difference in length rather than a difference in quality, and the lack of a quality difference will confuse the English-speaking listener.

2.12 *Perception and production of a phonemic difference through different structural interpretation.* Linguists are in disagreement as to the phonemic interpretation of English /e/ as in *bait* and /o/ as in *boat*. Pike analyzes them as unit phonemes but phonetic diphthongs, and Bloomfield, Trager and others analyze them as phonemic diphthongs.[4] Spanish speakers hear a difference between English /e/ as in *bait* and /ɛ/ as in *bet*. They correlate English /e/ with the Spanish diphthong /ei/ as in *seis* 'six,' and English /ɛ/ with Spanish /e/ as in *sé* 'I know.' They do not perceive a quality difference between the initial element of English /e/ and /ɛ/. This can be shown by deliberately holding steady the initial quality of English /e/ throughout the vowel of *bait* and contrasting it minimally with /ɛ/ as in *bet*. The Spanish speaker will have trouble hearing the difference, while the English speaker will not be disturbed in his perception of the difference. The Spanish speaker will make the transfer of his diphthong and his single vowel /e/ to English when he speaks as well as when he listens. English speakers listening to him hear his diphthong as English /e/ and his single vowel as English /ɛ/.

Conclusion: Regardless of the analysis we may favor, the contrast between /e/ and /ɛ/ and that between /o/ and /ɔ/ in English does not constitute a significant problem for speakers of Spanish learning English.

2.13 *Dialect differences and pronunciation problems.* All languages spoken by large numbers of people show variations called dialects. "Dialect" is used here to mean a manner of speaking showing pronunciations, words, expressions, and grammatical constructions used more or less uniformly throughout an area or a group of speakers, which manner differs from those of other speakers of the same language. Sometimes a given dialect

---

[4] For a discussion of these two different interpretations see Morris Swadesh, "On the Analysis of English Syllabics," *Language*, 23 (1947): 137-50; and Kenneth L. Pike, "On the Phonemic Status of English Diphthongs," *Ibid.*, 151-59.

has greater prestige than other dialects. Dialects are distributed over different geographic areas, among different social classes, and at different times in the history of a language. English at present has several dialects that have prestige and are therefore considered standard. In the United States there are at least three major dialect areas: the North, the Midlands, and the South. In the eastern states the boundaries between these dialect areas have been carefully determined through field interviews. The boundary between the North and Midland areas runs in a westerly direction through northern Pennsylvania. That between the South and the Midlands runs southwest along the Blue Ridge Mountains in Virgïnia.[5] In England there is the dialect of the south of England, which resembles Received Standard in pronunciation, and there are more northerly dialects whose pronunciation resembles Midland American more closely than does Received Standard. There are also standard dialects of the Scots, Australians, New Zealanders, etc.

Spanish has several accepted standard dialects also. The usual dichotomy made between Castilian and American Spanish is a false oversimplification. Castilian is a definable standard dialect, but American Spanish shows several dialects that do not coincide with national boundaries. There are several acceptable dialects in Spain itself, some of them showing close resemblance to American dialects.

Chinese scholars seem to assign uniformly greater prestige to Mandarin Chinese than to other varieties. If their attitude reflects actual prestige resulting from acceptance as the standard dialect, the situation is different from that for English and Spanish at the present time.

When faced with these differences, what can we do in the analysis of pronunciation problems? The answer is to compare a specific dialect of the native language with a specific dialect of the foreign language. The student proceeds in that fashion. He goes from his own native dialect to the foreign dialect of his model. If the analysis is going to predict and describe the problems he will find, it will have to compare those two dialects. When we need to know the problems facing speakers of more than one dialect, separate solutions must be worked out for each problem. If the differences are minor, it may be possible to combine the presentation of the problems, but the statements must remain quite specific. The same holds true if the analysis is to apply to more than one dialect of the foreign language.

---

[5] For a study of dialects and dialect boundaries see Hans Kurath, *A Word Geography of the Eastern United States* (Ann Arbor: Univ. Mich. Press, 1949).

Problem: Castilian Spanish has a phonemic contrast between /θ/ as in *cien* 'one hundred' and /s/ as in *sien* 'temple.' The speaker of Castilian Spanish and of other varieties that have the same distinction will therefore have no trouble with English /θ/ as in *think* and /s/ as in *sink*.

Other dialects of Spanish do not have a phoneme /θ/. Words which in Castilian are pronounced with the phoneme /θ/ are pronounced with /s/ in those other dialects. The speakers of these dialects, then, will have major difficulty with English /θ/ contrasted with /s/.

2.14 *Unpredictable alternation between two potential substitutions.* It is interesting that although, for example, Japanese, Thai, Tagalog, and some dialects of Spanish lack a phoneme /θ/ that might approximate English /θ/ as in *think,* Japanese and Spanish speakers substitute /s/ while Thai and Tagalog speakers tend to substitute /t/ instead. Why is there a difference if in all four languages there is an /s/ phoneme and a /t/ phoneme?

The answer, I believe, lies in the fact that the individual tends to transfer his whole sound system, and his whole sound system involves more than /s/, /t/, and the absence of /θ/. It will be helpful to try to explore some of the additional dimensions involved in this particular problem of /θ/, searching for a better understanding of what otherwise seems arbitrary, nonsystematic transfer of sounds.

English /θ/ as in *think* has as its form several phonemic features.[6] It is voiceless in contrast to /ð/ as in *then,* which is voiced. As to manner of articulation, it is a fricative in contrast to /t/ as in *ten,* which is a stop,[7] and in contrast to /s/ as in *sink,* which is a grooved sibilant.[8] As to point of articulation it is dental in contrast to /f/ as in *fin,* which is labio-dental. We can represent these contrasts, keeping the relative positions of the phonemes as they usually appear on phonemic charts, as follows:

---

[6] A phonemic feature is one which somewhere in the language is used as the only distinctive feature of sound between two phonemes.

[7] The stop feature of /t/ in contrast to the fricative feature of /θ/ is dominant over the difference in point of articulation between these two phonemes. The /t/ articulated with the tongue tip between the teeth, but still as a stop, remains /t/. And when the point of articulation is alveolar but /t/ is pronounced as a fricative, it becomes /θ/.

[8] Again, in the contrast between /θ/ and /s/, although there is a difference in the point of articulation as well as in the manner of articulation, the latter — fricative versus sibilant — constitutes the phonemic distinction. A fricative /s/ becomes /θ/, and a sibilant /θ/ becomes /s/, but a dental /s/ remains /s/, and an alveolar /θ/ remains /θ/.

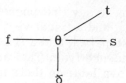

It is easy to see why a Spanish speaker chooses /s/ instead of /t/ as a substitute for /θ/ when he does not have the phoneme /θ/ in his dialect of Spanish. The Spanish speaker has undoubtedly met other Spanish speakers who do have a phoneme /θ/ and who use it in many words in which he uses /s/. He has heard /θien/, /kaθa/, etc., for the words *cien, caza,* etc., which he pronounces as /sien/, /kasa/, etc. The field of /θ/ when he speaks might be represented as empty.

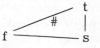

When he listens, it might be represented as follows:

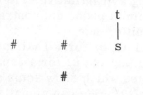

In listening, the features of /θ/ operate for him as /s/. It thus seems quite reasonable that he should substitute /s/ for /θ/ in learning English. He does. He says, "I sink so" /aɪ sɪŋk so/ when attempting to say "I think so" /ai θɪŋk so/.

It is not as simple to see why a Japanese speaker tends to use /s/ also as his substitute for English /θ/. The potential field of /θ/ for him is something like the following:

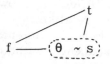

The symbol # appears where English /f/, /θ/, and /ð/ would be located. We can readily see why he does not substitute /ð/ or /f/; he does not have those phonemes in Japanese. But why does he substitute /s/ instead of /t/, both of which are separated by one phonemic feature from /θ/ and would therefore seem to be phonemically equidistant from it?

It might be tempting to say that phonetically the difference between a sibilant, [s], and a fricative, [θ], is less than the difference between a stop, [t], and a fricative, [θ]. But immediately one faces the evidence from Thai and Tagalog speakers, who also have /t/ and /s/ available in their native language but substitute /t/ and not /s/ for /θ/. With this evidence against us, we are quite happy to return to the general premise that differences are relative to the phonemic structure of each language, and we abandon the explanation of the Japanese choice as based on general phonetic proximity of sibilants and fricatives.

If we cannot find a convincing explanation of the Japanese speaker's choice of /s/ instead of /t/ we can at least leave the way open by seeking phonemic proximity and distance within the phonemic structure of Japanese. If we could show that within the structure of Japanese the difference between a sibilant such as /s/ and a fricative such as /θ/ has less phonemic "force" than the difference between a stop and a fricative, we could then say that a Japanese speaker uses /s/ for /θ/ in English because *to him* they are more alike than /t/ and /θ/. This would be obviously true, but we find it difficult to show evidence why in his system /s/ and /θ/ are more alike.

The evidence we find is not sufficiently strong to settle the matter completely. In Japanese we find one phonemic contrast in which a stop, /k/, contrasts minimally with /h/, which might conceivably be called a fricative and which in most of its variants is articulated in the region of /k/.[9] We do not find any minimal contrasts between a fricative and a sibilant.[10] There is then a slightly better chance that the Japanese speaker will hear a difference between English /t/ and /θ/ than between /s/ and /θ/ and that he will therefore tend to render English /θ/ as /s/ rather than as /t/.

We are introducing a quantitative criterion of difference based on the number of minimal phonemic contrasts attributable to a phonemic feature of difference.

The potential field of /θ/ for a Thai speaker does not seem to differ markedly from that of /θ/ for a Japanese speaker except for two other phonemes which show some similarity with it, namely Thai /f/ and /th/. We can visualize that field as follows:

---

[9]Before /u/ and before /t, k, č, š/ Japanese /h/ is usually a bilabial fricative. Before /u/ there is free variation between [h] and [f].

[10]The contrast between /s/ and /h/ involves the point of articulation as well as the manner of articulation.

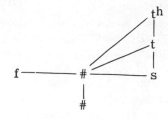

Since there is no minimal contrast between a labio-dental point
of articulation and an interdental one there would seem to be
some possibility that the Thai speaker might perceive and pronounce English /θ/ as /f/, but he chooses /t/ instead. The fact
that English /t/ has a variant with heavy aspiration should also
tend to associate his Thai aspirated /tʰ/ with English /t/, leaving
his unaspirated Thai /t/ to associate with English /θ/. This is
not a very convincing possibility, but it is sufficiently plausible
to show that the association of /θ/ with /s/ is less likely for a
Thai speaker than for a speaker of Japanese.

A Tagalog speaker tends to substitute his /t/ for English /θ/.
Tagalog has no fricatives so that Tagalog speakers have the same
lack of experience in distinguishing between a stop and a fricative,
/t/ and /θ/, as between a sibilant and a fricative, /s/ and /θ/.
The choice of /t/ must be on other terms. Spelling, the fact that
English /θ/ is spelled with *th* is sometimes adduced as a possible
factor. We leave the suggestion in the realm of possibility.

Although in the above situations we tried to illustrate cases
which showed a maximum of difficulty in analysis, one thing may
be of general value. ⌈When a phoneme in the foreign language does⌉
not exist in the native language the student will tend to substitute
the native phoneme that seems nearest within the whole structure
of his native language. In such cases, a difference is "greater"
when used in the native language as the minimal difference in the
largest number of contrasts between phonemes.⌋

Another observation should be made at this time. In the kind
of comparison we are presenting here there remain problems
that cannot be completely stated without actual observation of the
speech of informants as they attempt to learn the foreign language.
Experienced teachers who have listened to their students' pronunciation carefully may be able to decide which choice will be
made when the analysis remains ambiguous.

3. Problem Analysis: Stress and Rhythm.

    3.1 *Introduction.* The analysis of problems of stress and

rhythm is of importance not only because stress is phonemic, that is, significant, in English and in other languages but also because stress and rhythm usually exert considerable pressure on other matters of pronunciation. Compare for example the word *have* under varying degrees of stress: With zero stress on *have*, the sentence, "You have done it," becomes /yuv dɛ́n ɪt/, where *have* does not constitute even a separate syllable but is reduced to /v/. With minimal stress on *have* the sentence becomes /yu əv dɛ́n ɪt/, where *have* is reduced to /əv/, a syllable that is weaker in stress than /yu/ and much weaker than /dɛ́n/. With intermediate stress on *have* the sentence becomes /yu həv dɛ́n ɪt/, where *have* is reduced to /həv/, a syllable of equal stress as /yu/. With maximum nonemotional stress on *have* the sentence may become /yu hǽv dən ɪt/. Obviously we must consider stress and rhythm in any description of pronunciation problems.

Since we know that the learner tends to transfer his pronunciation system, including stress and rhythm patterns, to the foreign language we will look for stress and rhythm problems in the differences between the two languages. Let's describe briefly the stress and rhythm of English and Spanish. Once we have prepared these descriptions we will be better able to compare them in the work of locating and describing the problems that an English speaker finds in learning Spanish and those that a Spanish speaker finds when learning English. We must also touch on the pressure of stress patterns on segmental phonemes, and we will have to consider problems related to cognates and other types of words. The comparison of English and Spanish, although directly relevant only to those two languages, serves here to illustrate how two languages may be compared as to stress and rhythm.

3.2 *English stress and rhythm.* English has four significant degrees of stress, that is, four stress phonemes, or five if we consider zero stress as phonemic. Three of those degrees of stress are fixed as to position and are describable in terms of words or phrases; the fourth is movable and describable in terms of sentences and sequences of sentences. We will call the three word or phrase stresses *primary, secondary,* and *weak,* primary being the heaviest, secondary the intermediate one. We will call the movable stress *sentence stress.*

Let the word *substitution* serve as our example. When spoken rather slowly and somewhat deliberately, *substitution* often shows secondary stress on the first syllable, *sub-*, weak stress on the second syllable, *-sti-*, primary stress on the third, *-tu-*, and weak stress again on *-tion*. These three stresses are fixed as to their position or potential position in that particular word and in words and phrases that fall into the same stress and rhythm pattern. Primary stress may sometimes be reduced in rapid speech, but if present it will normally be on the same syllable. The particular pattern represented by the word *substitution* as described is a rather frequent one in English; other examples, in phrases as well as words, abound: *constitution, with the people, must accept it,* etc.

Secondary stress, which has given rise to arguments as to whether or not it constitutes a phonemic entity, may be reduced to weak stress in rapid speech or it may be exaggerated to become primary stress in precise speech or in insistent, high-pressure style. Radio announcers often increase secondary stress to the level of primary stress and thus multiply the number of attention peaks in their delivery. However, a secondary stress cannot replace the normal primary stress in the same word or phrase except under the effect of sentence stress contrasting that syllable with some other one. For example, the word *constitution* is possible with two primary stresses, *cónstitútion,* but it is not normal with primary on the first syllable, *con-,* and secondary on the third, *-tu-,* except under contrastive sentence stress. An example of this exception would be the contrast, "I said CONstitution, not SUBstitution," capital letters indicating the sentence stress. Even here, however, it may occur that the syllables *-tu-* preserve their primary stress. In any case, it is important to note that secondary stress is relatively infrequent in English compared to primary and weak stresses. It is also important to note that many speakers seem not to use secondary stress at all but have a system of weak, primary, and sentence stresses instead.

Sentence stress. The sentence "What did you understand?" may occur with a sentence stress on any of its four words.

> WHAT did you understand?
> What DID you understand?
> What did YOU understand?
> What did you underSTAND?

Sentence stress is readily recognized in contrastive position:

> I said NOW, not next YEAR.
> I know what YOU said, but what did HE say?
> Did you say THE letter or just A letter had come?

To say only that the position of sentence stress depends on the context does not actually describe the structure involved. In short sentences the sentence stress usually coincides with the last primary stress:

I'm going to study in Ann ARbor.

In a series of sentences or phrases in which part of the material remains the same, the sentence stress falls on the parts that change:

JOHN is in school.
MARY is in school.
JANet is in school.
EVerybody's in school.

We had a vacation in Florida.
We SWAM in the sun.
We PLAYED in the sun.
We RAN in the sun.
We BASKED in the sun.
We had a wonderful time.

There may be more than one sentence stress in each sentence:

Getting MARried is one of the most important things that HAPpens to you.

Sentence stress is used to tie specific parts of sequence sentences and response sentences[11] with sentences that have been uttered previously. The following is one of several possible readings:

She went downstairs to the door and BECKoned to him.
"You have taken them aWAY?"
"YES, ma'am."
"Why did you DO it?"
"I saw you looking at them too LONG."
"What has THAT to do with it?"
"You have been HEART-broken all the morning, as if you did not want to LIVE."
"WELL?"
"And I could not BEAR to leave them in your way. There was MEANing in your LOOK at them."
"Where are they NOW?"

---

[11]Sequence sentences are "all the single free utterances or sentences, after the one at the beginning," in a stretch of continuous discourse on the part of one speaker. "Some of the utterance units *began* conversations.... All the other utterance units occurred after the conversation had started. They occurred as *responses* to preceding utterance units... The utterance units of the second group, those that occurred after the conversation had started, I have called 'response utterance units.'" Charles C. Fries. *The Structure of English* (New York: Harcourt, Brace, and Co., 1952), pp. 241, 37.

"Locked UP."
"WHERE?"
"In the STAble."
"GIVE them to me."
"NO, ma'am."
"You reFUSE?"
"I DO. I care too MUCH for you to give 'em up."
                      (Thomas Hardy. *The Return of the Native*.)

Emphatic stress. A sixth degree of stress may be recognized
(counting zero stress as one of the degrees) if we grant separate
phonemic status to emphatic stress. This stress is characterized
by much louder and much longer rendition of the syllable which
carries it. The amount of loudness varies according to the degree
of emotion involved and may reach the level of a shout. I am in-
clined to recognize this kind of stress not as a separate "emic"
entity in the stress system but as a voice qualifier which is not
restricted to the syllable receiving the stress.

Authors occasionally italicize words for special emphasis.
This special emphasis may at times represent emotionally
charged emphatic stress:

"Jane!" Mrs. Baxter cried, "you *mustn't* say such things!"
                      (Booth Tarkington. *Seventeen*.)
"My father *killed* somebody?"
                      (George Santayana. *The Last Puritan*.)
"If I could *help* you in any way..."
                      (Sinclair Lewis. *Main Street*.)
"*Why* should I love you?" "*Why* should I?"
                      (Elizabeth. *The Enchanted April*.)
"Now we shall be *completely* happy!"
                      (Elizabeth. *The Enchanted April*.)

But in other examples it seems to be sentence stress in a position
where it would not normally fall:

"Why did they trouble *him* that way?"
                      (Harvey Allen. *Anthony Adverse*.)
"Marise, my darling, I want always to do what is best for *you*
to do."   (Dorothy Canfield. *The Brimming Cup*.)
"...that — rich people had hearts, and that women *were* sis-
ters."   (Katherine Mansfield. "A Cup of Tea.")

English rhythm. English stress rhythm is characterized by a
primary stress in each phrase, and accompanying secondary and
weak stresses, with a tendency to achieve approximately the same

length of time for each phrase regardless of the number of syllables involved.[12] Sentence stress is superimposed on this rhythm
pattern and adds sentence rhythm as well.

The syllable receiving heaviest stress shows greater length
than the others especially when a sentence stress coincides with
it.[13] This emphasis and length of stressed syllables and the
tendency to uniform length between stresses makes English
rhythm "phrase timed" rather than "syllable timed."

The poetic practice of giving secondary stress to all weak
syllables, which also tends to equalize their length, results in a
special effect, the connotation of concentrated thought and feeling
that characterizes much of English poetry. This difference in
connotation is achievable precisely because the normal, matter-
of-fact rhythm is so different.

3.3 *Spanish stress and rhythm*. Spanish has three significant
levels of stress in nonoratorical, nondeclamatory style. Two of
those levels are describable in terms of words and phrases; their
positions are fixed for each word. The third stress is describable in terms of sentences; it is movable within the sentence to
signal different points of attention. The word *constitución* shows
a heavy stress on the last syllable and less pronounced stress on
the other syllables. We will call the heavy stress *primary* and
the less heavy one *secondary*. The movable stress describable
in terms of sentences will be called *sentence stress*.

An acute accent mark will symbolize primary stress, the absence of any stress mark will indicate secondary stress, and a
syllable written in capital letters will indicate sentence stress.

Although Spanish syllables receiving primary stress or sentence stress are longer than other syllables they are not as long
as similar syllables in English. Spanish rhythm tends to give
each syllable approximately the same duration of time. The
phrases will thus be proportionately longer or shorter depending
on the number of syllables they contain. Spanish, therefore, may
be said to have syllable-timed rhythm. Actually, there are differences in the length and energy of syllables with secondary
stress, but the differences are minor and seem to depend on distance from the primary stresses.

---

[12]This Procrustean characteristic of English rhythm may explain in part why syllable
boundaries and the definition of the syllable have remained such a baffling problem for
American linguists. Some linguists have even refused to recognize the syllable as a
structural unit at all even though in some languages, at least, it may be an easily describable unit of distribution of phonemes and stress.

[13]For a somewhat different analysis of English stress see the widely known analysis by
George Trager and Henry Lee Smith in their *Outline of English Structure* (Norman, Okla.:
Battenburg Press, 1951).

All differences in stress are relative, not absolute; they are identifiable not in absolute physical units of measurement but in relative terms in comparison with other stresses in the same utterance.

For special effect a secondary stress may be increased to the level of a primary stress in any syllable except the one preceding a fixed primary stress: compare *cónstitución, constítución,* but not normally *constitúción.* To raise to primary stress the syllable preceding normal primary stress, it is necessary to impose a contrasting sentence stress on it. Primary stress then may be further described as not permitting a higher stress in another syllable in the same phrase.

Sentence stress in Spanish falls on the last primary stress with hardly any noticeable difference in resulting emphasis. *¿Cómo está usTED? ¿Cómo le VA? Buénos DIas. ¿Qué TAL?*

When sentence stress is placed on some other word for special or contrasting emphasis, the difference is more readily observable.

> *¿COmo está ustéd?*
> *¿COmo le vá?*
> *BUEnos días.*
> *¿QUE tál?*

Authors occasionally use italics to signal the special placing of such a sentence stress:

> ¿Es que podemos creer *demasiado* a Dios?
> ¿Podemos confiar *excesivamente* en el Padre?
> ¿Podemos en esta tierra amar *con exceso* a Cristo?
> (Jesús Urteaga Loidi. *El valor divino de lo humano.*)
> No podemos separarlos, porque Dios *no quiere* actuar solo,
> y el hombre..., no es que no quiera ..., es que *no puede.*
> (Jesús Urteaga Loidi. *El valor divino de lo humano.*)

3.4 *Comparison of English and Spanish stress.* Since Spanish does not have a weak stress and since we know from experience that the student transfers the system of his native language to the foreign language, we conclude that English speakers learning Spanish will tend to use weak stress in most syllables which require secondary stress in Spanish. They will also tend to lengthen beyond the pattern of Spanish the syllables receiving primary and sentence stress.

We see that there will be no difficulty in the production of secondary stress as such, but there will be phonemic substitution of weak stress for secondary stress in one direction, English to

Spanish, and secondary for weak in the other, Spanish to English. And there will be phonetic difficulties with primary and sentence stress in the lengthening of Spanish stressed syllables by English speakers and shortening of English stressed syllables by Spanish speakers.

Changes in segmental phonemes resulting from changes in stress. It is a regular feature of English to modify the pronunciation of utterances as the speed of talk or length of phrases increases, so that progressively more syllables are reduced to weaker stress. Compare for example the series of changes in the same sentence under different degrees of reduction.

> *He can understand them.*
> /hí kǽn əndərSTÁEND ðém/
> /hì kə̀n əndərSTÁEN dəm/
> /hìkn əndrSTÁENəm/
> /hìknənrSTə́Nəm/

We see that /i/ is reduced to /ɪ/; /æ/ to /ə/ and eventually to zero in some places; /-nd/ + open transition to /-ndəm/ and eventually to /-nəm/.

When an English speaker learning Spanish changes secondary stress into a non-Spanish weak stress, he also introduces reductions of words which render them non-Spanish. For example, Spanish *benemérita* /be-ne-mé-ri-ta/ may be pronounced as non-Spanish /bɛ̀n-ə-mɛ́r-ə-tə/.

Conversely, when the Spanish speaker learning English gives secondary stress to weak-stressed syllables, he substitutes for the weak-stressed vowels /ə,ɪ/ or the omitted vowels one of the five full vowels of Spanish.

Special problems resulting from sequences of stresses. In addition to differences in the number of stress phonemes and their phonetic characteristics, Spanish and English show differences in the sequences in which the stresses occur. In words of Latin origin in English the position of primary stress is often describable in terms of the suffixes and the number of a syllable when counted from the last one in the word: *constitution, substitution, addition, invention, suspicion, decision,* for example, are stressed on the next to the last syllable.

Other words in English tend to have primary stress on the first syllable if they have no prefix, and on the second if they begin with a prefix: *shovel, civil, water,* stressed on the first, and *debunk, detract, dehorn, deduct,* stressed on the second. The fact that the latter examples are all verbs does not detract from the point being made: that English has definite patterns in the placement *what about* ~~nouns-project contract etc.~~

of primary stress and that some of those patterns are describable from the beginning of words and others from the end.[14]

Spanish also shows definite patterns in the placement of primary stress, but the location seems to be governed from the end of the word.

Problem: Spanish speakers learning English seem to discover this pull of English primary stress toward the beginning of words. They show this by overextending the pattern and pronouncing the word *museum* with stress on the first syllable. They may even find it difficult to pronounce the word with stress on the second syllable even though in Spanish they actually pronounce *museo* that way and would only have to transfer their Spanish pattern to place the primary stress where it normally falls in English.   *related by descent- same root*

Problem: Cognate words show patterns of correspondence in the placement of primary stress. These correspondences are a factor in the difficulty or ease of the pronunciation of those words. Spanish words ending in *-ción* have a primary stress on that last syllable. English cognates ending in *-tion, -cion* /šən/ are stressed on the syllable preceding that suffix. Spanish speakers learning English will first attempt to pronounce these words with stress on the last syllable and having failed to get the correct pronunciation will next attempt to pronounce them with stress at the beginning. Once a few words in this pattern are learned, however, they will manage others with great ease.

Spanish words ending in *-al* are stressed on the last syllable; English cognates ending in *-al* are stressed on the antepenult syllable: Spanish *capitál, animál, decimál* correspond to English *cápital, ánimal, décimal*. English speakers learning Spanish will attempt to stress these words on the first syllable, and when this is found to be incorrect, they may attempt to stress the second syllable. Once a few words are learned with primary stress on the end syllable, others will fall easily into pattern.   *third syllable counting from the end.*

These patterns of correspondence in the words of the two languages constitute a distinct problem. The difficulty will usually be the difference in the location of the primary stress.

Problem: Spanish words ending in *-dad* are stressed on the last syllable. English cognates ending in *-ty* are stressed on the antepenult syllable: Spanish *habilidád* corresponds to English *abílity*. Spanish speakers learn this pattern of correspondence early and they apply it even if they have never consciously

---

[14]This is an obvious oversimplification of the data available. We are merely illustrating this type of language patterning.

understood it. From Spanish *posibilidád* they may produce English *possibílity*. They then apply the pattern to the cognate *difficulty* which does not follow the same pattern of stress and they invent the form *diffículty*.

4. Problem Analysis: Intonation.

4.1 *Location and description of intonation problems.*

Intonation versus tone. Pitch, the voice quality we describe as high or low on a musical scale, is used in two distinct ways in language: (1) as part of the sentence and phrase, and (2) as part of the word. English uses voice pitch as part of the sentence and phrase but not as part of the word. Chinese, on the other hand, uses voice pitch as part of the word. The pitch, or tone, is as much a part of a Chinese word as are the sound segments; changing the tone can change one word into another word. The pitch of a word in English, as we said, is not part of the word; the pitch in English changes to meet the needs of the phrase and sentence and the word remains the same. When pitch is used with phrases and sentences, we call it intonation. When pitch is used to identify and differentiate words, we call it tone. Chinese is a tone language. English is not a tone language; it is an intonation language.

The problems of learning the pitch system of a foreign language will vary depending on whether both the native and foreign languages are intonation languages or one is a tone language. To illustrate the various types of problems that arise we will discuss examples involving intonation alone, and intonation and tone. In any case, many of the suggestions given above for the comparison of sound segments can be adapted to pitch analysis as well. Since English will be one of the languages compared in the illustrations, it is helpful to begin with a sketch of English intonation.

4.2 *English intonation.*

Four pitch phonemes. We know that English has four pitch phonemes, not four fixed points on a musical scale but four relative levels.[15] The intervals between them change in amplitude

---

[15] Kenneth L. Pike postulated these four phonemes of pitch and describes them in his book, *The Intonation of American English* (Ann Arbor: Univ. Mich. Press, 1945), the most complete treatment of English intonation. Pike uses numbers to represent the four pitches, number 1 to represent the highest pitch and number 4 to represent the lowest. He also uses lines, solid, dotted, or a combination, above and below the line of print to represent the pitches. In the pronunciation materials of the English Language Institute the solid lines were used for pedagogical reasons. For a full treatment of these pitch phonemes see Pike's Chapter 3, "General Characteristics of Intonation," pp. 20-43. For a simple discussion of the findings see Charles C. Fries, *Teaching and Learning English*

from speaker to speaker and from situation to situation even for
the same speaker. In the sentence, "He's a student," spoken with
a normal *mid pitch* at the beginning, a *high pitch* on *stu-* and dropping to a *low pitch* at the end, we hear three of those four pitches
in operation. A woman would normally render the same sentence
at a higher general pitch than a man. And both would raise the
level of the pitches and widen the height of the intervals under
various circumstances, for example when attempting to communicate with someone across the street. They would lower the
pitches and keep them close together when speaking to someone
next to them in a dentist's waiting room.

The level of the pitches is not steady but wavers considerably
within an utterance, or to put it another way, there are variations
within each pitch level as the sentence progresses. These variations within each pitch level seem to correlate in part with variations in stress and with particular sound segments, but have no
primary significance in communication. A sound spectrogram of
our sample sentence, "He's a student," with intonation as described above, was made in such a way that the harmonics of
the voice are clearly shown. Tracing the tenth harmonic from
the sound spectrogram produced the line shown on the chart.[16]
Professor Gordon Peterson gave the following information concerning the chart:

For the voiceless consonants the vocal cords normally do not vibrate and thus these
consonants have no fundamental voice frequency. Also, it is often difficult to identify the
overtone structure in voiced consonants with strong friction. These considerations largely
account for the breaks in charts of the fundamental voice frequency by the sound spectro-
graph.

In complex waves such as those for the vowels and voiced consonants of speech, the
overtones are integral multiples of the fundamental. Thus the fundamental voice frequency can be plotted by tracing one of the harmonics and dividing the frequency scale by
the corresponding harmonic number. It has been demonstrated that the perception of the
pitch of a complex wave is influenced by its overtone structure. Since there is greater
emphasis in the energy of the higher formants of front vowels, the pitch of a high front
vowel might seem higher than that of a high back vowel at the same fundamental voice
frequency. It follows that there is not an exact correspondence between fundamental voice
frequency and perceived tone and intonation, but the correspondence is usually sufficient
to be of aid in determining linguistic structure.

---

as a Foreign Language (Ann Arbor: Univ. Mich. Press, 1945) pp. 20-23. George L. Trager
and Henry Lee Smith, Jr., confirm the four-pitch system of English in *An Outline of English Structure* (Norman, Okla.: Battenburg Press, 1951) but number them 4 for the highest and 1 for the lowest.

[16]Professor Gordon Peterson kindly provided the sound spectrogram and the tracing of
the tenth harmonic to show intonation level. In many spectrograms which we made of a
sentence in the various intonation patterns used in this section, it became abundantly
clear that the pitch of the voice does not jump from one "level" to another, but glides
more or less sharply toward points which are heard by native speakers as minimal differences. Much remains to be done in the instrumental study of intonation within a
structural frame. *See* "Phonetics, Phonemics and Pronunciation: Spectrographic Analysis," by Gordon Peterson, Monogr. No. 6 (1954), *Georgetown Univ. Monogr. Series on
Languages and Linguistics*, pp. 7-18.

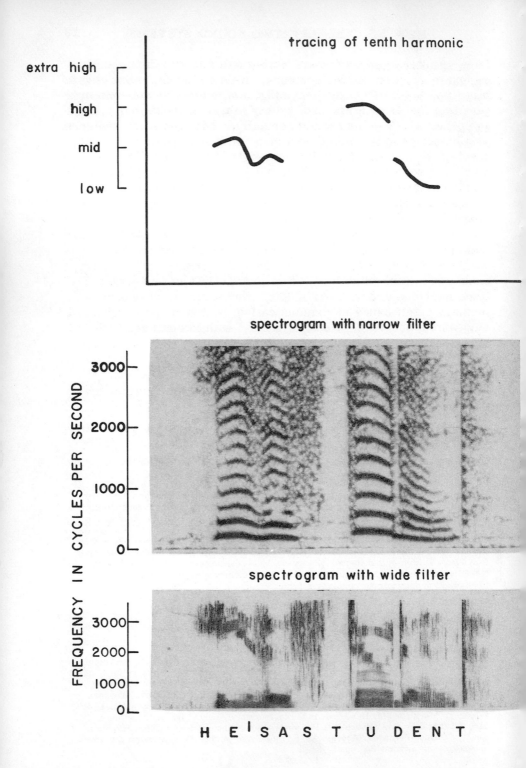

tracing of tenth harmonic

extra high
high
mid
low

spectrogram with narrow filter

FREQUENCY IN CYCLES PER SECOND

3000
2000
1000
0

spectrogram with wide filter

3000
2000
1000
0

H E ' S A S T U D E N T

In spite of these variations in the relative level of these pitches, the startling fact remains that they operate as the only four significant pitch units, or phonemes, in English. Representing these levels with the letters *l* for low, *m* for mid, *h* for high, and *x* for extra high, we can illustrate the four pitches in contrast at the end of the same example:

He's a STUdent. (A normal, matter-of-fact report.)
m   h   l

He's a STUdent. (Indicating that the utterance is not finished
m   h   m   or that the fact that he is a student is like
an afterthought, having significance for
something said previously.)

He's a STUdent. (Indicating mild doubt as to his being a stu-
m   h   h   dent or as if trying to remember if he is a
student.)

He's a STUdent. (Indicating strong disbelief or surprise.)
m   h   x

Intonation phrases. We have shown the four pitch phonemes of English in intonation phrases rather than in isolation because they normally occur and operate in phrases. The situation is somewhat similar to that of segmental phonemes such as vowels and consonants, which also operate in sequences such as words and morphemes, and not in isolation. Not all the pitch evidence is relevant to the identification and operation of intonation phrases. Two points are usually sufficient to identify the phrase: the pitch phoneme at the onset of the phrase or sentence stress, and the final pitch. Those are the pitches marked on the word *STUdent* in the examples above. When there is a fall and a rise between those two points, a third pitch is required to identify the phrase, namely the pitch at the point where the fall changes to a rise. It is possible to write then

STUdent
h l   m

indicating a glide from high to low and then a rise to mid.

In addition, when there are syllables before the onset of phrase stress, the intonation phrase has an introductory pitch there also, as in our examples above, which had a mid pitch at the beginning. This introductory pitch is not essential to the phrase, because its occurrence is mechanically determined by the existence of syllables preceding the phrase or sentence stress. Notice the following examples in which the intonation

phrase is a high—low, meaning matter-of-fact report with attention on *student*.

What is his occupation?   STUdent.
                                 h-   -l

What is he?   A STUdent.
                                 m h-   -l

What did you say he was?   Hè's a STUdent.
                                 m   h-   -l

If the onset of stress occurs on *he* instead of on *stu-*, the center
of attention is shifted to *he*, but the intonation phrase continues to
be high—low, meaning in this case again 'matter-of-fact' report.
Compare
                    Hè's a STUdent.
                    m   h-   -l

                    HE'S a stùdent.
                    h-   -l

The hyphens tie together the central, essential part of the intonation phrase as above: m h- -l, h- -l.

Some intonation phrases of English.   The intonation phrases of
American English are numerous.   Below are some of the more
common ones.[17]

Phrases falling to low.   High—low, mid—low, extra high—low.
The general meaning of falling phrases is one of contrastive
pointing.   Examples,

High—low: He's a STUdent. (Matter-of-fact attitude.
                   m   h-   -l   Attention on student.)

Mid—low: He's a STUdent. (Detached attitude.)
                   m   m-   -l

Extra high—low: He's a STUdent. (Intensely contrastive,
                   m   x-   -l   surprise.)

Phrases falling to mid.   High—mid, extra high—mid.   The
general meaning is contrastive pointing as for other falling
phrases.   Those ending on mid, however, rarely if ever occur
before a final pause and as a result they also imply nonfinality.
Examples:

---

[17]A much fuller treatment of these and other intonation phrases is given in Pike, *The
Intonation*, Chap. 4, "Specific Contours," pp. 44–106.

High—mid: He's a STUdent. (Showing mild doubt and
                   m   h-   -m   or nonfinality.)

Extra high—mid: He's a STUdent. (Showing intense surprise
                   m   x-   -m   or doubt, and incomplete-
                                     ness as in a question.)

Phrases rising from low. Low—mid, low—high, low—extra
high. All rising phrases tend to indicate incompleteness, the incompleteness of a conversation, of a series, or of a question that
requires an answer.

He's a STUdent.   (Deliberative. Detached incompleteness.)
m   l-   -m

He's a STUdent.   (Matter-of-fact incompleteness. Thoughtful
m   l-   -h   doubt.)

He's a STUdent.   (Surprise; strong doubt. Deliberation.)
m   l-   -x

Phrases rising from mid. Mid—high, mid—extra high..

He's a STUdent.   (Matter-of-fact inquiry.)
m   m-   -h

He's a STUdent.   (Surprise and disbelief.)
m   m-   -x

The meanings of these latter intonation contours are elusive and
difficult to define, but they do contrast. The meanings given may
be restricted to the particular pattern of utterance used as illustration, as for example in the mid—high, given as matter-of-fact
inquiry. The same intonation phrase coming in the middle of a
sentence might signal a series.

Although a rising intonation, especially a mid—high, is often
used with questions, a falling intonation such as a high—low is
also used with questions of all types. The intonation meaning will,
of course, be different, but the questions will remain questions.
Compare a mid—high and a high—low on the question "What?" in
the following contexts:

"I did it again."

"What?"
m- -h

"I did it again."

With the rising intonation, the meaning is something like 'What did you say? I did not hear you.' With a falling intonation the meaning is quite different:

"I did it again."

"What?"
h- -l

"I forgot my dental appointment."

The meaning is now 'What did you do? Please explain.' Both the falling and the rising intonations can be used on questions which can be answered with "yes" or "no". Compare for example,

"Are you a STUdent?"   (Polite. The first question of a con-
m   m-   -h   versation.)

"Are you a STUdent?"   (Business like, matter-of-fact. One
m   h- . -l   in a series of questions but perhaps
                        not the first one.)

4.3 *Comparing two intonation languages.* The simplest case in a comparison would seem to be that of two intonation languages; for example, English and Spanish, or English and French. In such cases there will be two stages in the comparison: (1) comparison of pitch phonemes, and (2) comparison of the intonation patterns.

Stage 1: Comparison of pitch phonemes. We have seen that English has four distinct pitch phonemes, which we called low, mid, high, and extra high. These pitch phonemes have no lexical meaning in themselves, but any one of them can change an intonation phrase into another, just as any one of the segmental phonemes of English can change one word into another word. If English is the foreign language, we will inquire how many pitch phonemes the native language has. It may have four, three, two, five, or perhaps even some other number.

Same number of pitch phonemes. If the native language has four pitch phonemes, and if they are similar to the English pitch phonemes in level, we can assume that the speakers will have no particular difficulty hearing and producing the pitch phonemes of English. According to my information, that is the case of English and Spanish, in which both languages have four pitch phonemes that can be labeled as low, mid, high, and extra high.[18]

[18]My interpretation of Spanish intonation as a four-pitch phoneme system is based on the data presented by Tomás Navarro Tomás in *Manual de entonación española*, (2d ed., rev.; New York: Hispanic Institute in the United States, 1948). J. Donald Bowen in "A Comparison of the Intonation Patterns of English and Spanish" (*Hispania*, 39, No. 1, March, 1956, 30-35) limits the system to three pitch phonemes: low, mid, and high. Bowen recognizes a high pitch phoneme in matter-of-fact questions and in emphatic statements. If that is the case, we need to recognize an extra high pitch phoneme in emphatic questions.

The fact that two languages have the same number of phonemes and that they are similar enough to function as "same" in the two languages does not indicate that there will not be problems in learning their intonation. As we will see later, there are major problems in learning the intonation patterns that are different in form or different in meaning. That kind of problem will be discussed in stage 2, when we compare intonation patterns.

Different number of pitch phonemes. Problems will arise when the native language has fewer pitch phonemes than the foreign language. If the native language has three pitch phonemes and the foreign language has four, we can predict a learning problem. Two possibilities are worth mentioning in such a case: first, the three pitch phonemes of the native language coincide with the lowest three pitch phonemes of the foreign language. Since there is no counterpart for the extra high level of the foreign language, the problem will be to learn to hear and to use the extra high pitch phoneme as distinct from the high one and to distinguish the extra high from emotional variations.

In the second possibility the total range of the three pitch phonemes of the native language is the same as the total range of the four foreign ones, that is, the high and the low phonemes of the native language range as high and as low as the extra high and the low of the foreign language. The problem then will be learning to hear and to produce two pitch phonemes in the middle range where the native language has only one. An additional problem may turn out to be the distinction between high and extra high and between mid and low.

When the student goes from a native language having more pitch phonemes than the foreign language, there will be no major intonation problem, because he will be able to hear the fewer distinctions of the foreign language. Once the simpler system has been understood by him, he will be able to use it without much effort. He will tend, however, to have erroneous secondary reactions such as, for example, feeling that the people who speak that language are cold and detached, not very expressive, or feeling the opposite, that they are overly emotional and excitable, and the like.

Stage 2: Comparison of intonation patterns. Even when the pitch phonemes of the two languages are the same in number and similar in pitch, problems will undoubtedly arise in learning the intonation patterns. These problems are caused by intonation patterns in the foreign language that do not exist in the native language or by patterns that are similar in form in the two languages but have different meanings.

When an intonation pattern in the foreign language is not found in the native language we can assume that the student will have trouble producing and hearing it. He will hear it as some other pattern which does exist in the native language. It may sometimes appear on the surface that he does not hear one of the pitch phonemes, and in effect he may actually have trouble with only one pitch phoneme in the pattern, but a more accurate diagnosis is one that correctly restricts the problem to that particular pattern since he will not have trouble with the same pitch phoneme in other patterns.

Most of the intonation problems will stem from patterns which are the same in form in the two languages but have a different meaning in each. The student automatically selects the pattern of his native language for the meaning he is going to express. He also interprets the foreign language problem with the native language meaning.

Problem: Spanish uses a rising mid-high intonation pattern on the confirmatory attached question *¿verdad?* For example, *Es interesante ¿verdad?* meaning, 'It's interesting, isn't it?' which in English has a falling high-low intonation on *isn't it.* Lexically, Spanish *¿verdad?* with its rising intonation, and English *isn't it* with its falling intonation are quite similar.

Spanish speakers learning English will transfer their rising intonation pattern into English in the above example as elsewhere. The tendency is so strong that a student may fail to produce the falling pattern even after the sentence is repeated for him and his attention is called to it. As an informal experiment a student who used a rising intonation in such an attached question was asked to imitate a teacher who kept repeating it with a falling intonation as the model. The student attempted to imitate the falling intonation pattern twelve consecutive times and failed. The experiment can easily be repeated with results that vary but still reveal a problem.

Problem: Spanish matter-of-fact statements are normally said with a low-mid-low intonation pattern. The mid pitch begins at the first stressed syllable and changes to low at the onset of the last stressed syllable. English matter-of-fact statements, on the other hand, are normally said with a mid-high-low intonation pattern, with the high occurring at the last stressed syllable. As a result, Spanish speakers will tend to give English statements with the low-mid-low pattern of Spanish, producing an unintentional effect of detachment. Going in the opposite direction, English speakers learning Spanish tend to rise to high on the last stressed syllable as they would in matter-of-fact English. The result in Spanish, however, is either a question or an emphatic statement, neither of which are intended by the speaker.

4.4 *Comparing a tone language and an intonation language.* English and Spanish, even though their systems are different, are both intonation languages. But when one of the languages is a tone language, for example when one of the languages is Chinese or Thai, the comparison becomes more complex and the problems of the student learning the other language are probably greater. The experience of Thai and Chinese students learning English testifies to the difficulty of English intonation problems for those speakers. The experience of English speakers learning Chinese also attests the great difficulty that learning Chinese tone represents for them in turn. Some never learn it even when they live in China many years.

In making a comparison of the systems of a tone and an intonation language we will have to consider not only differences in pitch but entirely different systems of distribution of pitch. In English, as we saw above, pitch is distributed over phrases and sentences. In Chinese and in Thai it is distributed over morphemes and words. A high—mid sequence in the middle of a sentence in English does not attach to a particular word as such, but to the position in which that word occurs. Similarly, a high—low sequence at the end of a sentence does not belong to the word at the end of that sentence but to that position itself. The very same words will have different pitch elsewhere. In Thai, however, the high tone of a given word belongs to that particular word, that is, the tone serves to identify the particular word, to distinguish it from other words. Consequently, a Thai speaker learning English expects pitch to attach to morphemes and words, and he is lost because English to him keeps changing the tones hopelessly as far as the individual word is concerned. Similarly, an English speaker learning Chinese does not perceive tone as part of morphemes and words, and of course he cannot produce it as such. He is thoroughly confused by the seemingly unpredictable changes in the "intonation" of the sentences.

The comparison of a tone language with an intonation language will involve the same two stages as when both languages were of the intonation type. The first stage is the comparison of the minimum significant pitch units, the pitch phonemes. The second stage will be the comparison of patterns of pitch-phoneme sequences. In comparing the pitch phonemes we must discuss separately those tone languages in which the pitch phonemes are level and those in which the pitch phonemes are not level but gliding. Those with level phonemes of pitch are called register tone systems, and those with gliding phonemes are called contour tone systems.

Comparisons involving register tones only. Several cases may arise involving register tones and intonation. The comparison at this first stage will parallel that between two intonation languages. We can take up two cases separately as illustrations.

Case A. One language has two tones, and the number of pitch phonemes of the other language is four: low, mid, high, and extra high. There will be a serious problem when the speaker of the tone language tries to learn the intonation of the other. Both high and extra high pitch phonemes will be heard as "same" by him. Mid and low will also be heard as same. There will probably not be trouble in hearing the difference between mid and high. The difficulty will also include speaking. The student may not be able to produce the extra high and the low pitch phonemes if the range of his two native tones is narrow. Or he may sometimes interchange high and extra high, and low and mid if the pitch range of the two native tones is wide.

A student going from a four-pitch phoneme system to a two-tone system will not have any major difficulty learning the tones, and may only have to overcome the tendency to jump at secondary interpretations about expressiveness, emotionalism, or the lack of it, which more than likely have no basis in fact.

Case B. If one of the languages has three significant tones and the other has four pitch phonemes, we can make the same analysis as when comparing two intonation languages, one of which has three pitch phonemes and the other, four.

Comparisons involving contour (gliding) tones and level pitch phonemes of intonation. When the language has gliding tones rather than level ones, the analysis may be more difficult but we can still chart some expected things to clarify the problem. By way of illustration we can assume a tone language with two gliding tones — a rise and a fall — and an intonation language with four pitch phonemes — low, mid, high, and extra high. Going from the language with the two gliding tones to the four-pitch phoneme language, the student will hear the level pitch phoneme system as if it were a system of glides. He will hear clearly the difference between a rise and a fall but he will not hear the difference between the lower pitch phonemes or the higher ones. Thus he will not hear the difference between a rise from low to mid and from mid to high or between a fall from high to mid and one from mid to low. The problem is then to learn to hear and to produce the level pitch phonemes as significant units of patterns, which at first he hears only as undifferentiated rises and falls.

The second stage involves comparison of tone and intonation patterns. The most important problem here is the difference in distribution between tone and intonation. In the tone language, as we have seen, the pitch belongs primarily to the word, whereas in the intonation language, it does not belong to the word but to the phrase and sentence. In listening, the speaker of a tone language learning English, for example, will attribute the pitch variations to the words and will end in complete confusion as to the tone he hears. In one utterance he will hear the word *leaves,* for example, with a falling high—low pitch; in another he hears it with a level mid pitch; he will hear it with a rising mid—high intonation and with level low or level high, etc. He will hopelessly try to remember the pitch pattern of *leaves* but will fail because *leaves* as a word has no pitch pattern in English. Going in the opposite direction, that is from intonation into tone, an English speaker learning the tone language is equally baffled because he will be listening for intonation patterns on the phrases and sentences.

Complicating the data is the fact that tone languages usually have an intonation system over and above the tone system of its words. The intonation system of tone languages tends to be a simple one limited to two additional pitch phonemes occurring at phrase and sentence final points. When the additional pitch phonemes resemble those of the foreign language, they will be transferred without difficulty and will simplify the learning burden. For the English speaker learning the tone language they further complicate the learning problem by (1) misleading him to assume that he is learning the pitch patterns of the language, and (2) making the description of word tone more complex, since tone is modified at phrase and intonation ends.

The discussion on comparison of intonation and tone systems has included few examples because intonation has only recently been described in structural terms. There is a scarcity of structural data on the intonation of specific languages. As structural descriptions of the intonation of other languages appear, it may be possible to find concrete examples illustrating the above and other important problems.

4.5 *Problems of juncture and word boundaries.* In learning a foreign language one of the problems is the identification of the constituents of utterances. One of the important constituents of utterances is the word. Words have to be identified as words for their lexical meaning, and words have to be identified as members of form classes for the grammatical functions they perform and the grammatical meanings they convey in the utterance.

The identification of words is a matter of pronunciation as well as of vocabulary and grammar. A Brazilian journalist studying English complained after a test of aural comprehension that his difficulty was not in pronunciation but in the vocabulary of the test. He felt he did not know enough words. Arguments to the contrary failed to convince him that pronunciation had been at least part of the difficulty. He was ready to abandon pronunciation to devote more time to vocabulary. As a last resort I showed him the test that had troubled him and let him read the items he had missed when listening to them. Through reading he was able to give the expected answers to many of those same items. Obviously, having to grasp the units of the language through the medium of sound had been his difficulty. This same experience can be reproduced over and over again with unfailing regularity.

We identify words through sound segments, stress, and tone in tone languages, and also through word boundaries. The importance of these boundaries may be more easily admitted if we note a difference between the way words are joined in speech and the spaces left between words in present-day writing in many languages. Identifying word units in reading has been made easier by that practice. Notice that it is more difficult to read the following sentences because the words are run together. "Wedonot realizethatinspeakingwemaynothaveasclearlydefinedwordjunctures asthespacesbetweenwordsinwritingwouldhaveusbelieve. Spaces betweenwordsarehelpfulinidentifyingwordsinwrittenmaterial."

In the spoken language, word boundaries are sometimes identified by the presence of permitted sequences of phonemes at the beginning and at the end of words. In Spanish, /sp/, /st/, /sk/ are not permitted at the beginning or end of words; a vowel has to precede them initially or follow them finally. Examples of their use initially after a vowel or finally before a vowel are numerous: *escuela, aspecto, estudiante, escudo, obispo, esto, casco,* etc. A person who has studied Spanish and hears /vanestandobien/ is ready to separate words as /van estando.../, /vanes tan.../ or /van es tan.../, but not as /vane stand.../, because /st/ is not permitted initially without the vowel. In English, however, /st/ does occur initially in many words: *student, school, Spanish,* etc. and so an English speaker listening to that Spanish utterance will have the interference of potential units such as /stand/, which is common in his native sound system but not permitted in Spanish.

Word boundaries are also marked in part by the transition — juncture — between sounds at such boundaries. The transition between the /t/ and the /r/ in *eat rye* is different from the transition between the same two sounds in *we try*. If we represent the more open transition by a space we would have something like /ìt rái/ vs. /wì traí/. The same kind of difference is observed in slow pronunciation of the well known example, *night rate* vs. *nitrate:* /náɪt rèt/ vs. /náɪtrèt/. Linguists are not completely in agreement in the analysis of these transition phenomena. In these particular examples the different phonetic articulation of the /r/ is quite obvious: in /náɪtrèt/ it is a fricative sound, almost a sibilant; in /náɪt rèt/ it is a retroflex. In other cases of difference in transition it may not be as simple a matter. In any case, however, we must agree that transition phenomena are important in identifying words.

Word boundaries are often leveled or shifted in rapid speech when they are fitted into syllable units that do not coincide with the word boundaries. The utterance, *Attend it,* for example, may be pronounced /ətɛ́nd ɪt/ with a word boundary between *attend* and *it* as expected, or it may be pronounced /ətɛ́n dɪt/ with the word boundary, if any, forced over to the syllable transition between /n/ and /d/.

When word boundaries are marked by the same sequences of segments and the same transitions in the foreign language as in the native language, we do not expect any major learning problem. If the boundaries are differently marked we can expect difficulty and will attempt to describe the differences in the analysis of difficulties.

The problem may be particularly acute for speakers of languages like Chinese, which have mostly single syllable words with strongly marked boundaries, when they learn a language with a variety of word lengths and with shifting transition boundaries. When such speakers learn English, for example, they have considerable difficulty in identifying the word units in actual utterances, because of the variety in the length and structure of English words and the less obvious word boundaries, and because of the changes they undergo with different styles of pronunciation. In reading, on the other hand, the difficulty is obviated by the standard practice of leaving spaces between words.

This problem of boundaries is observable not only among foreign speakers of a language but in child language as well. My three-year-old daughter used two word formations in Spanish which are of interest here. She said *suvítas* with an initial /s/ for the word *uvitas* 'little grapes' or simply 'grapes' in child language. And she said *savelítas* with an added initial /sa/ for the word *velitas* 'little candles' or simply 'candles.' She said, *¿Dónde hay *suvítas? Yo quiero *suvítas,* meaning 'Where are there grapes? I want grapes,' and she said, *¿Dónde hay *savelítas?*

*Yo quiero *savelitas,* meaning 'Where are there candles? I want candles.' She had heard *uvitas* and *velitas* in utterances such as *¿Quiéres uvitas? ¿Quiéres más uvitas? ¿Quiéres las uvitas? ¿Quiéres tus uvitas?* etc. with /s/ preceding *uvitas*. In Spanish the most frequent syllable pattern is that of a consonant plus a vowel. Compare the consonant plus vowel beginning of other words she heard: *peritas, manzanitas, sopita, comidita, zapatitos,* etc. She identified the word for grapes as *suvitas* probably because, having heard the /s/ preceding *uvitas* in close transition with it, she placed the word boundary before the consonant, following a dominant Spanish pattern.

The case of *savelitas* seems equally interesting. She heard *tus velitas, las velitas,* with /s/ before the *v* of *velitas* in rapid transition, but *sv* does not occur initially in Spanish words, so she normalized it into a Spanish pattern by adding a vowel between the *s* and the *v*, giving *savelitas* on the pattern of *suvitas, sopita,* etc.

Pauses. Languages usually end their utterances, sentences, and sometimes their phrases with distinctive features of sound, length, and silence, and these features vary from language to language. English has a final pause characterized by a fading out, a lower or dropping pitch, and silence. It has been symbolized in many ways. We will use a period /./ to represent it, with the understanding that this is a special use of the period, independent of any other conventional use of that symbol. English also has a tentative pause characterized by a sustention of the end pitch and at times a lengthening of the last syllable preceding the tentative pause. It will be represented as a comma /,/, again with the proviso that this is a special use of that symbol. Still a third type of pause is presented by some linguists; a slight rise before silence. It may be symbolized as /?/, also with the understanding that this is a technical use of the question mark independent of any meanings it may have acquired through conventional use of the question mark in ordinary writing.

Utterances, sentences, and sometimes phrases are also begun with special features of sound articulation, length, or reduction of length of initial sounds, in the breaking of silence. Thus far no contrastive initial pauses have been reported by linguists for English, and we will not use any symbol for the initial features of utterance.

When differences exist between two languages in the form, the meaning or the distribution of these pauses and transitions, there may be problems involved in learning the other language. Some varieties of Mexican Spanish tend to unvoice the final syllable before a final pause. Transfer of that pattern to English produces major changes in the intonation patterns of English.

Chapter 3

HOW TO COMPARE TWO GRAMMATICAL STRUCTURES

1. Introduction: What Does Grammatical Structure Mean?

1.1 Because of early overemphasis on memorization of
grammatical rules as an end-all of language learning, and the
reaction against that extreme which has resulted in an equally
disastrous negation of all grammatical study nowadays, it is necessary and helpful to clarify what is meant by grammatical structure and what is not meant by it.

1.2 *Not grammar as definitions or as grammatical terms in
the older sense.* Some might think that by grammatical structure
we mean grammar, and in a sense that is true, but there are a
number of things that grammar often implies that we do not mean
by grammatical structure, certainly not from the point of view of
language learning problems. Grammar sometimes means giving
traditional definitions to elements of speech, definitions that do
not account for the facts of language.[1] The type of problem that
results from that kind of grammar requires the student to define
a noun, a subject, a direct object, or it requires him to write N
above the nouns, V above the verbs, D O above the direct objects
in given sentences. Since many native speakers of a language are
unable to define or even identify by technical terms the grammatical elements of their native language, we cannot accept that kind
of problem as representing the task of learning a foreign language.

1.3 *Not absolute rules of correctness.* Another aspect that
grammar sometimes has and grammatical structure does not is
that of artificial "correctness," found in many handbooks. This
correctness point of view assumes that grammar is a set of absolute rules to which the language must adjust. The attitude is
that these rules were laid down by some authority who based
them on reasons which we need not understand and which we cannot question. When a speaker or writer uses language that is not
in accord with these fixed rules, the correctness point of view
assumes that he is guilty of bad grammar regardless of accepted

---

[1]Charles C. Fries, *The Structure of English* (New York: Harcourt, Brace, and Co.,
1952), *passim.*

usage among educated native speakers.[2] In that point of view, when applied to the analysis of grammatical problems in learning a foreign language, it would be considered a problem if the student did not use grammar which "ought" to be used by native speakers rather than that which is actually used. For example, the traditional rules of *shall* and *will* in English would be considered a problem, and the foreign speaker learning English would be considered wrong if he used *will* with the first person, in spite of the fact that educated native speakers use *will* with the first person, and their speech is accepted.[3]

1.4 *Not usage as merely usage.* Does grammatical structure mean usage then, that is, does it mean what people actually say as opposed to what some grammar books rule they ought to say? Grammatical structure deals with the things people say, but it means more than the mere recording of examples of usage. The usage point of view does not give us criteria to decide which matters of usage are significant in communication and which are not; it does not tell us how to locate those elements that are part of the signaling structure of the language, that signal its structural meanings. The usage point of view results in "problems" that require the student to decide if this or that turn of phrase is the best one, regardless of whether or not the difference is structurally important in communication. An unusual turn of phrase such as *He is capable to go* might be considered just as incorrect as a phrase like *a watch pocket,* used when the speaker wishes to mean 'a pocket watch.'

1.5 *Grammatical structure as matters of form that correlate with matters of meaning.* We mean by grammatical structure the systematic formal devices used in a language to convey certain meanings and relationships. The word order of *is* before *he* in the sentence *Is he there?* spoken with a falling high—low intonation is the signal for one type of question in English.[4] If a foreign speaker does not react to that sentence as a question he may be

---

[2]C. C. Fries, "The Rules of the Common School Grammars," *Publications of the Modern Language Association,* Vol. 42 (March, 1927). S. A. Leonard, *The Doctrine of Correctness in English Usage, 1700-1800* (Univ. Wis. Studies in Lang. and Lit., Vol. 25, 1929).

[3]C. C. Fries, "The Periphrastic Future with Shall and Will in Modern English," *PMLA,* 40 (1925), 963-1024. See also *American English Grammar* (New York: D. Appleton-Century Co., 1940) pp. 150-167.

[4]A rising mid—high intonation is often used in English for other types of questions, for example to ask for a repetition of information just given. By using a normal falling high—low intonation with *Is he there?,* the same intonation we usually use in the statement *He is there,* we no longer have intonation as a clue to the question and thus leave the word order arrangement as the signal.

missing the structural significance of the word order arrangement. To describe the grammatical structure of English is not to describe every observable feature of usage but to describe those features that systematically convey meanings and relationships. The difference between the mere recording of usage and grammatical structure is parallel to the difference between phonetics and phonemics. In phonetics we are interested in describing all observable sound features in a language; in phonemics we describe those units that are significant.

2. Illustrative Discussion of Elements of Grammatical Structure and Types of Structural Items.

2.1 *Form and Meaning.* In the description of grammatical structure we mentioned form and meaning. Any structure, or pattern, as we will often call a unit, is assumed to consist of form and meaning, for example, *book: books, idea: ideas, heart: hearts.* The meaning of this contrast in English is 'one' versus 'more than one,' that is, singular versus plural. The form is the "-s" ending [-s, -z, -ɪz] for the plural and the omission of the ending for the singular. The omission of the ending is referred to as a zero ending, in order to indicate that it is significant in contrast to the "-s."

2.2 *Elements of form used in grammatical structures.* It is important to keep in mind that a variety of formal devices may signal grammatical meanings. And it is this variety that causes many of the learning problems in mastering a foreign language, since the use of different devices by two languages will constitute a problem.

Among the most frequent elements used in various languages to signal grammatical structure are word order, inflection (bound morphemes), correlation of forms, function words, intonation, stress, and pauses.

2.2.1 *Word order as a grammatical signal.* In English *Can he come,* with a falling high—low intonation, signals a question in contrast to *He can come,* which is a statement.[5] In Spanish, *Guantes de lana para niños* means a reasonable 'Wool gloves for children,' but the same words in a different order, *Guantes para niños de lana,* would mean a humorous, 'Gloves for wool children.' The Spanish function word *de* makes the noun following it a modifier of the one preceding it, position certainly being significant

---

[5]See Fries, *The Structure of English,* for an analysis of English sentence patterns.

here. Again in English, *pocket watch* is not the same as *watch pocket* since the modifier-head relationship is signaled by position in English: whichever word comes first becomes the modifier. In *pocket watch,* the second word, *watch,* is the head of the construction, and *pocket* becomes the modifier. In *watch pocket* the roles are reversed.

     2.2.2 *Inflection as a Grammatical signal.* Inflection is a very common grammatical signal, and one that has traditionally been studied as grammar. In English, the "-s" ending to signal plural, as in *book: books.* The "-ed" ending to signal preterite in verbs as in *jump: jumped, call:called.* In Spanish, the *-o* ending to indicate first person singular of verbs, contrasting with other endings such as the *-ar, -er, -ir* of the infinitive as in *amo: amar, salto: saltar, llamo: llamar, veo: ver, subo: subir,* etc.

     2.2.3 *Correlation of form as a grammatical signal.* In English, the correlation of the inflection "-s" in verbs with a third person singular subject such as *he, she, it, John,* etc. For example, *I know: he knows: she knows: it knows: John knows,* to signal a sentence nexus, a subject-verb construction, in contrast to a modifier-head construction. Note the following contrast:

     A marriage promise...
     A marriage promises...

Compare also the following:

     The *list* of the books which *is* good... (The list is good.)
     The list of the *books* which *are* good... (The books are good.)
     The lists of the *men who* are good... (The men are good.)

The correlation of form between *list* and *is* in the first example is the signal that *list* is the antecedent of *which.* The correlation between *are* and *books* in the second example signals that the antecedent of *which* is *books.* In the third example the correlation between *who* and *men* helps us to recognize the fact that the men are good, not the lists.

     2.2.4 *Function words as grammatical signals.* Compare the series of parallel examples, *John came; He came; The boy came; Who came,* all spoken with the same high--low falling intonation pattern. The last one, *Who came,* is a question signaled by the word *who.*

     The same is true in Spanish in this type of question. Compare *Juan vino,* 'John came'; *¿Quién vino?* 'Who came?' In the second sentence, *Quien* 'who' signals the question. Many other languages signal this particular type of question by means of a function word which can be equated with *who* in this context.

2.2.5 *Intonation as a grammatical signal.* An intonation rise from mid to high signals a special type of question in English. Notice that the word arrangement is that of statements in these examples:

Questions: He's a student?   Statements: He's a student.
    m   h-   -h   m   h-   -1

    He lives there?   He lives there.
    m h-   -h   m h-   -1

Compare the following two types of questions signaled by a difference in intonation:[6]

Do they have a car

What

I said do they have a car

There may be arrangements just a little outside of the city that are possible

What

Oh, a lake cottage that could be insulated

2.2.6 *Stress as a grammatical signal.* Notice the different position of the sentence stress and the accompanying difference in meaning:

ConSIDer it.   (Give the matter some thought, don't dismiss it lightly.)

Consider IT.   (Give some thought to the word *it*, not to something else; or, of course, give some thought to whatever the word *it* represents here, but with emphasis on *it* in contrast to something else even if not mentioned in the utterance.)

Consider the PROBlem. (Give the problem, not something else, some thought.)

---

[6]Examples from Fries, *Ibid.*, p. 155. The intonation is represented by the line drawn through the question word *what*. When the line appears just below the type it represents a mid pitch. Directly above the type it represents a high pitch. Farther above the type it is extra high, and far below the type it is a low. A slanting line represents a glide to the next pitch. A vertical line would represent a sharper rise or drop between pitches. Fries omitted the punctuation purposely.

The position of primary stress may signal a form class difference:

(a) présent	(to) presént
(a) súbject	(to) subjéct
(an) óbject	(to) objéct

2.2.7 *Pause as a grammatical signal.* Notice the change in the modification structures when the tentative pause, signaled by a comma, changes position. Notice also that the intonation pitches and the stresses remain the same for each word individually.

Twenty , THREE-cent stamps (Twenty stamps, 3 cents each.)

Twenty-THREE , cent stamps (23 stamps, one cent each.)

Compare also the following examples:

A red WINE, barrel (The wine is red.)

A red , WINE barrel (The barrel is red.)

Again the position of the tentative pause seems to determine whether *red* modifies *wine* or *barrel.*

Contrasts like those above indicate that the position of a tentative pause is part of the grammatical signal and that it outranks intonation and stress — at least in some instances — as a signal of modification constituents.

In the following examples notice that although the pitches and the stresses are altered, the modification remains the same as long as the position of the tentative pause remains the same.

With tentative pause after *red:*

A RED, wine barrel (not a green one. The barrel is red.)

A red , WINE barrel (not a water barrel. The barrel is red.)

A red, wine BAR rel (not a bottle. The barrel is still red.)

With tentative pause after *wine:*

A RED wine, barrel (not a white-wine barrel. The wine is red.)

A red wine , BAR rel (not a bottle. The wine is still red.)

3. Grammatical Structure, a System of Habits.

3.1 *System*. In the examples used above we were able to isolate and contrast grammatical patterns one by one as if they were independent items with no relation to one another. The fact of the matter is that each pattern, each structure, contrasts not just with one other pattern but with many others. It is a complex net of these contrasts which constitutes a system for each language. Each pattern has a number of features which are the same as some features of other patterns and different from others. Compare the following few examples from English.

> He showed us the light house.
> He showed us the house light.
> He showed us a light house.
> He showed us the light houses.
> She showed us the light house.
> He has to show us the light house.
> He'll show us the light house.
> He shows us the light house.
> Did he show us the light house?
> Show us the light house.
> Don't show us the light house.
> Who showed us the light house?

Each example on the list above illustrates a potential change in the original simple sentence. The potential expansions are even more varied than the changes. Compare just one example:

> The man who is standing over there on the deck showed
> (He)   (showed)

> some of us who are not sailors and are fearful of being lost
> (us)

> the light house that they say is at the entrance of the bay, . . .
> (the light house)

In all of these examples, in addition to potential changes and expansions there are things which cannot change in English but might normally change in another language. The *the* does not change for number or gender; *light* does not change for number when it is a modifier, and it does not change for gender, the verb *show* does not change for number except in the present tense — *he shows, they show* —, etc., etc.

When one realizes that the average human being — any normal human being — handles such a system with ease, and with it the delicate sound, intonation, stress, and pause contrasts, the thousands upon thousands of words and word meanings, and he handles it all in everyday conversations and with any number of possible intentions, we are struck with wonder at the greatness of the gift of language, a gift which, among all the earthly creatures of God's creation, is given only to man.

3.2 *Habit.* In practical terms we understand that the use of a grammatical structure by a speaker depends heavily on habit. It would be well nigh impossible to think consciously of all the potential changes, expansions, and restrictions in uttering even a single sentence and still speak with anything approaching normal conversational speed. The average speaker of a language has from early childhood reduced practically all the operation of his grammatical system to habit. His attention as he speaks is squarely on his stream of thought and on the reaction of his listeners, and only very slightly on some features of his grammatical constructions. We simply do not realize the strength and the complexity of the habit system we have acquired through all the years of daily use of our native language.

4. Problems in Learning a Foreign Grammatical Structure.

4.1 *Transfer.* We know from the observation of many cases that the grammatical structure of the native language tends to be transferred to the foreign language. The student tends to transfer the sentence forms, modification devices, the number, gender, and case patterns of his native language.

We know that this transfer occurs very subtly so that the learner is not even aware of it unless it is called to his attention in specific instances. And we know that even then he will underestimate the strength of these transferred habits, which we suspect may be as difficult to change when transferred as when they operate in the native language.

We noted above (2.1) that the grammatical structures of a language have form and meaning. The example given was the plural inflection in English, with "s" as its form and 'more than one' as its meaning. It is important to add now that every structure has distribution, that is, it occurs in certain situations or environments and does not occur in others. In English the "s" plural occurs in noun heads as in *books, telephones,* etc., but it does not occur in modifiers of noun heads as *good* in *good books,* or *telephone* in *telephone books,* etc. In some other languages a plural inflection does occur in modifiers of nouns as well as in nouns. The point in bringing up this matter of distribution is that

in transferring a native language structure the learner transfers
its distribution as well as its form and meaning.

4.2 *Similarity and difference as determiners of ease and
difficulty.* Since even languages as closely related as German and
English differ significantly in the form, meaning, and distribution
of their grammatical structures, and since the learner tends to
transfer the habits of his native language structure to the foreign
language, we have here the major source of difficulty or ease in
learning the structure of a foreign language. Those structures
that are similar will be easy to learn because they will be transferred and may function satisfactorily in the foreign language.
Those structures that are different will be difficult because when
transferred they will not function satisfactorily in the foreign
language and will therefore have to be changed.

We can say that the degree of control of these structures that
are different is an index to how much of the language a person
has learned.

4.3 *Production versus recognition.* The effects of native language transfer are not identical when the learner speaks the foreign language and when he listens to it. When he speaks he
chooses his meanings and then produces the forms that in the
native language would signal those meanings. In listening, he
hears the forms and attaches the meanings they would have in his
native language.

Although on the surface it may seem that the effect should be
the same, when we look at specific examples we see that a difference exists. Take the English utterance *Can he speak English?*
The omission of the third person "s" ending on *speak* — compare
he speaks — is a problem for many students. They include the
"s" in the question, saying, **Can he speaks* ... instead of *Can he
speak. . . .* This is only a speaking problem, however, not a listening one — a production problem, not a recognition one — since
when native speakers omit the "s" the learner will recognize the
question equally well.

4.4 *What constitutes "difference" and therefore difficulty as
to form.* When a grammatical meaning is the "same" in two languages, for example, 'modifier,' 'subject,' 'statement,' the form
that signals it may be different on two levels. The lesser difference remains within the same "medium," for example function
words, inflection, word order, to be found between different
items: a different function word, a different inflectional ending,
or a different word order. The greater difference goes from one

medium in one language to a different medium in the other language; for example, function words in the native language but inflection in the foreign language, or word order in one language but a function word in the other, etc. It will be worth-while to consider specific cases in some major types of differences as to form.

4.4.1 *Same medium, different item: Function words.* The function word *who* in the utterance *Who came?* is approximately equivalent to the Spanish function word *quien* in ¿*Quién vino?* 'Who came?' An English speaker learning Spanish has to learn a new item, *quien*, in the same medium, function words, to signal the same meaning, 'question.'

Often the problem is more complicated because it involves other differences as well. The English function word *do* placed before the subject signals a question in the pattern illustrated by the example, *Do you understand?* The Japanese function word [ka] also signals a question in [wakari masu ka] 'Do you understand?' A Japanese speaker learning English expects to find a function word equivalent to [ka] and he finds it in *do,* but only in part. English *do* plus its position before the subject constitutes the signal for question — compare *do you* 'question' versus *you do* 'statement.' In Japanese the position of [ka] is fixed at the end of the sentence and therefore the word order is not significant in the same sense. The learning burden to the Japanese speaker studying English, then, will not only be that of learning a new item, *do,* a function word, but also using a different medium, word order. This latter difference constitutes the greater problem.

4.4.2 *Same medium, different item: Word order.* English one-word modifiers precede the head in a modification structure, and in general that position constitutes the signal of modification with class 1 as head.[7] For example, a *garden flower* is a flower, but a *flower garden* is a garden. Phrases used as modifiers usually follow the head, for example, *a man with a toothache* is a man. In Chinese, word order is also the signal for modification, but modifiers precede the head, whether they are single words or

---

[7]This is an oversimplified statement. For a description of the modification structures of English see Fries, *The Structure of English,* Chap. X; see Chap. XII for an analysis through immediate constituents. See his Chaps. V and VII for a description of class 1 words. Class 1 is marked, for example, by "determiners" (*the, a, every, no, my,* etc.), by inflection correlating with number, by the genitive inflection, by use in certain structural positions, by certain contrasts in form (*-tion, -ness, -ance, -ment, -er,* and others), etc. Examples of class 1 words are *meal, cooker, heating* (of a house), *combination, business,* etc.

phrases.[8] Thus a Chinese speaker learning English has to learn to place after the head those modifiers that are phrases or clauses. Conversely, an English speaker learning Chinese has to learn to place before the head those modifiers that are word groups.

The problem of the Chinese speaker learning English is greater than that of the English speaker learning Chinese because the Chinese speaker goes from a one pattern system — all modifiers precede the head — to a two pattern system — some modifiers precede and some follow the head. This greater difficulty can be thought of as parallel to the pronunciation problem of going from one phoneme, say Japanese /i/, to a two-phoneme contrast like /i ɪ/, *beat:bit*, in English. Going from the two-phoneme contrast of English to the single phoneme in Japanese is definitely less of a learning problem. As for grammatical structure problems, we also note that even going from the one pattern of Chinese to the two patterns of English would be less difficult than other cases in which modification may be signaled by word order in one language and sometimes by word order and sometimes by intonation in another.

4.4.3 *Same medium, different item: Correlation of forms.* The correlation of an "-s" inflection in the verb in English, as in *runs, jumps,* with singular form in the subject, e. g., *the car runs, the cars run,* is a problem for Spanish speakers who have a correlation of forms that operates differently. In Spanish the plural form of the subject, *coches* 'cars,' with its "-s" inflection, correlates with an "-n" inflection in the verb: *el coche corre, los coches corren,* 'the car runs, the cars run.' The difference in form to be learned by the Spanish speaker, however, is within the same medium and therefore less of a problem than if another medium were involved.

4.4.4 *Different media: Word order in one language versus intonation in another.* The English question, *Are you a student?* spoken with a falling intonation is signaled by the word order *are you* in contrast to *you are* in the statement. In Spanish a similar question, *¿Es usted un estudiante?* is signaled by pitch, a high pitch on the last syllable or on the first and last, depending on style. The word order is not significant since we can say *¿Usted es un estudiante?* for the same question. Intonation is the signal for question or statement, as can be proved by saying the sentence

---

[8] Yao Shen, "Two English Modification Patterns for Chinese Students," *Language Learning,* 1, No. 4 (1948), 19.

with a mid—low sequence at the end: the resulting sentence is heard by a Spanish speaker as a statement regardless of word order. In short, when we change the word order but keep the intonation constant, the kind of sentence does not change, but when we change the intonation, the sentence changes from statement to question and vice versa. In this case, the Spanish speaker has considerable trouble mastering the word order pattern of the English sentence, and the English speaker in turn has considerable trouble using the intonation pattern as the signal for the question in Spanish.

4.4.5 *Different media: Word order in one language versus function word in the other.* In Thai the function words /rў./ or /mǎj/ placed at the end of the sentence signal certain questions which in English are signaled by placing the verb before the subject. For example, the Thai question, /khǎw pen nákrien rў./ 'Is he a student?' contrasts with the statement, /khǎw pen nákrien/ 'He is a student,' only because of the presence of /rў./ in the question.[9] The word order of both question and statement is the same in Thai and is therefore not the signal for question or statement. In English the signal for that question pattern is the order of the words *is* and *he:* in the question, *is* precedes *he,* and in the statement, *he* precedes *is.* Compare *He is a student,* a statement with a high—low intonation pattern, and *Is he a student?* a question even with the same intonation pattern.

The English speaker learning Thai has difficulty learning to use a function word signal, /rў./, instead of his word order signal, *is he.* The Thai speaker has trouble using the word order signal of English for a pattern that he has been signaling with the function word /rў./ or /mǎj/.

4.4.6 *Different media: Word order in one language versus inflection in the other.* The indirect object, which is signaled in English by word order, is signaled in Latin by inflection. For example, in the English sentence *The daughter gives her mother a coat,* the position of *mother* tells us that she was the receiver of the coat. This can be proved easily by changing the order to *The mother gives her daughter a coat.* With the same words, stress, and intonation we now understand that the daughter, not the mother, was the receiver of the coat. Since the only formal difference in the two sentences is the change in the position of

---

[9]Kanda Sitachitta, "A Brief Comparison of English and Thai Questions," *Language Learning,* 5, Nos. 3 and 4 (1955), 130-34. The tone markings and the transcription in these examples follow those of the article. In the Thai alphabet on page 107 the /y./ of /rў./ is transcribed as ʉ: and the /j/ of /mǎj/ as y.

mother and *daughter,* we conclude that it is the position of the words that signals the subject and indirect object. In Latin, however, the same meaning is not signaled by word order but by the ending of the words. Latin *Mātrī fīlia vestem dat* does not mean 'the mother gives her daughter a coat' as might be guessed from the position of *mātrī* 'mother' at the beginning of the sentence; the sentence actually means 'the daughter gives her mother a coat,' and we understand this from the ending of *mātrī* (dative) and *fīlia* (nominative). The same words in the same order, but with different endings, *Māter fīliœ vestem dat,* changes the meaning to 'the mother gives her daughter a coat.' We thus see that it is the inflection of *māter* (nominative) and *fīliœ* (dative) that signals the subject and indirect object.[10]

The English speaker learning Latin finds a great deal of difficulty in grasping the subject and indirect object from the inflection of the words in the sentence.

4.4.7 *Different media: Function word in one language versus inflection in the other.* Spanish *iré* 'I will go' indicates future through inflection, and English *will go* indicates it by the function word *will.* Similarly Spanish *iría* 'I would go' indicates conditional by inflection, and English *would go* indicates it by the function word *would.*

Noncontrolled observations make me suspect that going from a function word signal to an inflection is more difficult than the reverse. There is reason to believe that such might be the case because even in the native language adults continue to learn new words long after their ability to learn new inflections and new sounds appears pretty well lost.

One also suspects that a formal device in the foreign language turns out to be easier if it is one of the media used significantly in the native language, though not in that particular structure. In other words, if inflection is used regularly as a grammatical signal in the native language, learning an inflection in the foreign language will be easier even in a structure in which inflection is not used in the native language.

4.5 *What constitutes "difference" and therefore difficulty as to meaning.* In the above cases we assumed that the meanings signaled in the two languages were in some way equivalent even if not identical. We went so far as to call them "same." The

[10]Waldo Sweet, "A Linguistic Approach to the Teaching of Latin," *Language Learning,* 4, Nos. 1 and 2 (1951-2), 42-53. The example is from Sweet's "Experimental Materials for the Teaching of Latin" (mimeo.), p. 36.

difficulty in such cases depended on differences in the formal
devices used in the two languages to signal the "same" meanings.
We now turn to cases in which a grammatical meaning in one of
the languages cannot be considered the same as any grammatical
meaning in the other language. This difference in two grammatical systems will constitute a learning burden and will therefore
be part of our attempt to predict and describe problems in learning a foreign language. A few examples will illustrate differences
in meaning.

Modern English has a remnant of gender in its grammatical
system as seen in the pronouns *he, she, it* and in classes of words
for which those pronouns may be substituted; thus *he* may be
substituted for the class represented by *man, father, uncle,* as
examples, but not for the class represented by *woman, mother,
aunt,* etc. Likewise *she* may be substituted for *woman, mother,
aunt,* etc. but not for *man, father, uncle,* etc. Finally, *it* may be
substituted for *chair, house, cloud* but not for the other classes of
words. There is, of course, some overlapping, but it is not relevant at this point. Spanish has a full gender system involving also
three genders — masculine, feminine, and neuter — as seen in the
pronouns *él, ella, ello,* in the articles *el, la, lo,* and in the classes
of words they determine or for which they may substitute. Compare *el hombre* 'the man,' *la mujer* 'the woman,' and *lo bueno* 'the
good (of something).' In spite of this outward similarity in the gender systems, it would be quite a mistake to assume that the three
genders mean the same thing in the two languages. The *it* gender
in English includes an enormously large class, whereas the neuter
gender in Spanish is restricted to a small class. The disparity in
these classes is so great that we cannot reasonably say they mean
the same thing.

Examples of different meaning as to gender are commonplace.
It in English; feminine in Spanish: *table: la mesa, house: la
casa, street: la calle, pistol: la pistola,* etc. *It* in English; masculine in Spanish: *book: el libro, dictionary: el diccionario,
floor: el suelo, revolver: el revólver,* etc. The speaker of English learning Spanish not only has difficulty remembering the
class to which each item belongs but finds it difficult to see why
mesa 'table' should be a "she" in the first place. He of course is
transferring the English meaning of the "she" class to the Spanish
feminine class as if the meanings were the same. A French
speaker on the other hand has no such difficulty with *mesa* because in his language the meaning 'feminine' is similar to that in
Spanish, and the item *la table* is classified the same as Spanish
la mesa.

Native speakers of English, Spanish, and the many languages

that have a meaning distinction between 'one' and 'more than one' (singular and plural) as a grammatical contrast in their substantives may tend to believe that all languages must make that meaning distinction. Yet we know that some languages make three number distinctions: 'one,' 'two,' 'more than two' (singular, dual, plural). Other languages made four number distinctions: 'one,' 'two,' 'three,' 'more than three' (singular, dual, trial, plural). And others make no grammatical distinction as to number at all.

In every case, languages can express the number involved, but when they have a number category in their grammatical system, as singular-plural in English, they have that meaning distinction in addition. English can express a specific number of things by means of a word or phrase: for example, *seven*, or *one thousand and one*. But in addition, we must classify these numbers into a meaning 'plural' when speaking that language. And in English the meaning 'plural' embraces any quantity from two to infinity; whereas in a language with singular, dual, and plural, the meaning 'plural' would be different in that it would not include two; it would include any quantity from three to infinity. When we find such differences in meaning between the native language and the foreign language we can assume that there will be a learning problem.

A more profound difference in what we have called meaning is the widely discussed observation by Whorf that in the language of the Hopi Indians there is no notion of time as we conceive it. We will quote Whorf *in extenso* here because the very notion of thinking without reference to time is difficult for us even to imagine. The reader who is struck by the significance of this observation by Whorf should refer to the article in which it appeared and to Hoijer (1954).[11] Needless to say that this difference in viewing the universe would constitute a serious obstacle for the Hopi Indian learning another language and for other speakers learning Hopi.

> I find it gratuitous to assume that a Hopi who knows only the Hopi language and the cultural ideas of his own society has the same notions, often supposed to be intuitions, of time and space that we have, and that are generally assumed to be universal. In particular, he has no general notion or intuition of TIME as a smooth flowing continuum in which everything in the universe proceeds at an equal rate, out of a future, through a present, into a past; or, in which, to reverse the picture, the observer is being carried in the stream of duration continuously away from a past and into a future.

---

[11]Harry Hoijer, ed. *Language in Culture* (Chicago: Univ. Chi. Press, 1954).

After long and careful study and analysis the Hopi language is seen
to contain no words, grammatical forms, constructions or expressions
that refer directly to what we call TIME, or to past, present, or future,
or to enduring or lasting, or to motion as kinematic rather than dynamic
(i.e. as a continuous translation in space and time rather than as an ex-
hibition of dynamic effort in a certain process) or that even refer to
space in such a way as to exclude that element of extension or existence
that we call TIME, and so by implication leave a residue that could be
referred to as TIME. Hence, the Hopi language contains no reference
to TIME, either explicit or implicit.[12]

4.6 *Problems caused by differences in distribution.* Sometimes a structure that constitutes no particular difficulty as to
meaning and form turns out to be a problem because of different
distribution in the two languages. A fairly neat example is the
plural inflection in Spanish and English. The meaning may be
considered the same in the two languages: 'more than one,' since
both English and Spanish have primarily a two-number system.
The form is similar: a sibilant ending, "-s" with variations.
The distribution, however, shows some sharp differences. The
Spanish plural inflection attaches to the noun head, the modifiers,
and the determiners. Compare the singular, *la paloma blanca*
'the white dove' with the plural, *las palomas blancas*. In English
the plural inflection attaches only to the noun head: *the white
dove : the white doves.* Because of this difference in distribution
the Spanish speaker will add a plural inflection to the modifier,
white, and the English speaker learning Spanish will tend to omit
the plural inflection in *blancas.* A parallel transfer occurs in the
article. Often, in addition to the difference in distribution, there
is a difference in the form as well.

5. Procedures in comparing two grammatical structures.

5.1 *General procedure.* We begin with an analysis of the foreign language and compare it structure by structure with the
native language. For each structure we need to know if there is
a structure in the native language (1) signaled the same way, that
is, by the same formal device, (2) having the same meaning, and
(3) similarly distributed in the system of that language. Let's
illustrate these points. Both English and German have the kind
of sentences we call questions. Both English and German use
word order as the signal in many questions. So far we have not
discovered any structural problem as to (1) formal device or

---

[12]Benjamin Lee Whorf, "An American Indian Model of the Universe," *IJAL,* 16, No. 2,
67.

(2) meaning. We note further that English uses the function word *do, does, did* before the subject to achieve the word order signal of that type of question. German does not use that device. We have thus found a problem as to (1) formal signaling device. We may expect a German speaker to say, for example, *Know you where the church is?* as a question instead of *Do you know where the church is?* He will simply be transferring the German pattern *Wissen Sie wo die Kirche ist?* which is similar to the pattern used with the verb *be* in English but not with the verb *know*.

Let's consider an illustration with Spanish as the native language. Both English and Spanish have the type of sentences we call questions. But questions which are signaled in English by means of word order are signaled in Spanish by an intonation contrast. We can expect trouble here since the Spanish speaker has learned to react to the intonation signal and to disregard the order of the words, which in his language is not structurally significant in this particular case. He has to learn to react to a different medium — word order — for the same structure. The German speaker had less of a task since his problem was simply to use a new word, *do,* in a medium — word order — which he already used in his native language to signal a question.

5.2 *More specific procedures.* In a signaling system less complex than human language, for example in the flag language used at sea, the above general procedure for comparison of two systems would be more than enough. In human language, however, the situation is much more complex, and we need to illustrate the procedure in greater detail.

First step: Locate the best structural description of the languages involved. Both descriptions should contain the form, meaning, and distribution of the structures. If the form, the meaning, or the distribution of a pattern is not described, or not adequately described, an attempt must be made to describe it accurately before proceeding any further.

Second step: Summarize in compact outline form all the structures. If English is one of the languages involved, we would describe the sentence types in it as questions, statements, requests, calls.[13] Under questions would be several patterns: questions with the verb *be;* questions with *do, does, did;* questions with *can, may, will,* etc. (function words of group B in Fries' classification[14]); questions with *when, where, why,* etc., plus reversal of word order; questions with *who, what,* etc., as subject;

---

[13] Fries, *The Structure of English,* Chaps. III and VIII.
[14] Fries, *ibid.,* Chap. VI.

questions with a mid—high intonation sequence regardless of word order; and other minor types of questions.

For each type, we need to know the inventory of formal signals at the sentence level. For questions with *be,* as for example *Is he a farmer?* the inventory would include (1) the form of *be* preceding the subject, (2) a sentence tie between *be* and the subject,[15] (3) a falling high—low intonation. We also need to know the structural meaning of this pattern, namely, 'to elicit verbal responses of the yes-no types (*yes; no; certainly; yes, he is;* etc.). As to distribution, this sentence occurs as a sequence sentence, that is, after another sentence has been said, in conversational style. We know this because it contains the sequence signal *he.* In situations in which the farmer of the example is in the attention of both speaker and listener, for example in a picture or present in person, *Is he a farmer?* can then also be used as a situation utterance, that is, at the beginning of a conversation. In literature, this same type of sentence may be used at the beginning of a work for a special effect, usually to arouse curiosity as to the identity of the *he.*

Also under sentence types should be described the types occurring as response utterances, that is, in response to a previous one. For example, *Home,* in response to *Where are you going?* or *Now,* in response to *When are you going home?*

In addition to the sentence types we need the parts of speech that constitute the elements of minimal sentences. The traditional eight parts of speech in English are more than can justifiably account for the elements of minimal sentences and too few to account for the variety of expansions of sentences used in English. Fries recognizes four parts of speech, which he labels with the numbers 1, 2, 3, and 4: class 1, *idea, tea, goodness, he,* etc.; class 2, *think, drink, be, enable,* etc.; class 3, *good, thoughtful, critical,* etc; and class 4, *well, thoughtfully, critically,* etc.

The outline should include function words used in expanded sentences. Fries identifies fifteen groups of function words. A few examples are given in italics in the following sentence: *The* small cloud *that the* men saw *on the* horizon *might not* be *a* cloud *but an* island.

The structure of modification, its various patterns, meanings, and distribution, must be included in the description. What is the formal signal that makes *sky blue* a color and *blue sky* the sky in English? Can *sky* as a modifier be used in all modifier positions or is it restricted in any way?

---

[15]Fries, *Ibid.,* pp. 144-45.

Word elements that are syntactically relevant, that is, part of the signaling apparatus of sentences, should be included. For example, elements that identify parts of speech, as the -s plural of *hats,* would be relevant to sentence structure.

Sentence stress, final pauses, tentative pauses, and intonation patterns complete the outline.

A similar compact outline of the other language would conclude the work of the second step.

Third step: Actual comparison of the two language structures, pattern by pattern. If English and Spanish are being compared we would find a question pattern in Spanish illustrated by *¿Es un campesino?,* literally, 'is a farmer?' but actually equatable to English *Is he a farmer?* which usually has a high—low intonation sequence. The inventory of formal signals of the Spanish pattern includes (1) the form of *ser* 'be' and (2) a rising intonation sequence from mid to high or a rise to extra high and a drop to mid or low, or some other sequence which is also an intonation signal for this type of question.

A comparison of the formal features reveals that (1) Spanish does not require the presence of a separate word for 'he,' while English does; (2) Spanish does not require a word order contrast with that of a statement, English does; and (3) Spanish requires an intonation signal which contrasts with that of statements, English does not. Problems as to form for a Spanish speaker learning English will then be (1) including a separate word, *he, she,* etc., as subject, (2) placing the verb *be* before the subject *he* to signal question, and (3) using a high—low intonation sequence instead of a rising one or an extra high—low (or mid) sequence as in Spanish.

An English speaker learning Spanish will have as his problems (1) remembering to omit a separate word for 'he,' which if included will produce a stilted "foreign" style, but will not by itself change the question to a statement; and (2) using the contrastive mid—high or mid—extra high—low (or mid) intonation pattern which actually signals the question in Spanish.

A comparison of the meanings reveals no major differences. In both languages a verbal response is elicited and the response is of a yes-no type; hence no problems will be expected here.

Comparing the structures as to distribution we find that in English the pattern discussed is restricted to the verb *be* and optionally to *have.* With other verbs the pattern is constituted by the function word *do* tied to the subject and preceding it. In Spanish the pattern discussed extends to all verbs. A Spanish speaker will thus have not only the problems of the form of the pattern as listed above but also the restriction of that pattern to *be* and optionally to *have*. This problem may also be stated as another case in which one pattern in the native language can be equated to two patterns in the foreign language. The problem of the English speaker learning Spanish is less severe since he will be going from two patterns into one.

Regrouping single problem patterns into larger patterns of difficulty. By comparing each pattern in the two language systems we can discover all the learning problems, but often the problem involved in learning one pattern is parallel to or actually the same as the problem in learning another pattern. It will make for economy and neatness to regroup the problems into larger patterns. In questions with *be* we saw that the problems of the Spanish speaker learning English would be: the reversal of word order, the inclusion of a subject pronoun, and the use of a falling, high—low, intonation. Upon analyzing questions with *can, will, may*, etc., we would find that the difficulties would be precisely those connected with *be*. These then are not two problems but one and the same problem applying to two patterns in English.

Analyzing questions with *do* we would find that the problem of the same Spanish speaker learning English would be (1) including the function word *do*, (2) a reversal of word order resulting from the position of *do* at the beginning, (3) the inclusion of the subject pronoun, (4) noninflection of the lexical verb, e. g., *he studies : does he study*, and (5) a falling, high—low, intonation in most instances. We see that part of the problem is the same as with questions with *be* and with *can, will* etc., namely the reversal of word order, the inclusion of a subject, and the use of a falling intonation.

Proceeding to questions with *when, where*, and *what, who(m), why*, not as subjects, we would find that the problems would parallel those of questions with *do* above except for the intonation, which in this case is also a falling, high—low, intonation in Spanish and would therefore not constitute a problem here. We would still have as problems (1) the inclusion of a function word, *do, can*, etc., (2) the reversal of word order, (3) the inclusion of the subject pronoun, and (4) noninflection of the lexical verb.

We could thus group these question problems into a larger pattern, involving word order and the inclusion of a subject pronoun in all cases. A falling, high—low, intonation would be restricted to some patterns, those eliciting a yes-no type of response. The noninflection of the lexical verb would be a problem in all but the pattern of questions with *be*.

5.3 *Separate descriptions of production and recognition problems.* Often, as illustrated earlier, the learning problem will not be the same when the learner attempts to speak the language and when he is merely listening. The tendency of Spanish speakers learning English to omit the subject pronoun in sentences, because in Spanish it is quite natural to omit it, is a problem only in speaking, in production. In listening, since English speakers will use the subject pronoun, there is no problem at all. It will therefore be necessary in the description of learning problems to label each insofar as it is a problem for production or for recognition or for both. In fact, the comparison will not be complete until both production and recognition have been explored for the kind of differences that constitute learning problems.

5.4 *Dialect differences and problems of style.* The grammatical structure of a language is best attested in spoken communication among the speakers of a language community. But even in the spoken language we observe variations regionally, socially, in different types of communication, and in individual styles. We do not use the same forms when speaking informally to our close friends as when addressing a stranger; we do not address all strangers the same way; we do not address a large unfamiliar audience the same as we address a small seminar of our own students, etc.

In written communication there are also wide differences depending on the type of communication and its style, and there are wide differences between written communication and the spoken language. In poetry, for example, the artist employs unusual patterns, altering the usual ones to achieve his purposes. Sometimes these stylistic variations are difficult to understand, and even highly literate native speakers find it necessary to read a poem many times to achieve a full grasp of its import. Short stories and other literary material also exemplify the special use of patterns that help achieve an artistic effect.

Plays are made up of conversations and are therefore often useful in getting at the spoken language, but we must not forget that in the conversation of plays the artist's object is not to write conversations but to achieve a literary effect, and he is apt to choose his patterns or rearrange them to suit his legitimate artistic needs.

Newspaper style is one of the least representative of the whole language. It is highly specialized, with standardized sentence types that are useful primarily for journalistic writing.

These literary and journalistic patterns have to be considered only when our purpose is to sample problems arising from specialized style.

What can we hope to do in view of the great complexity of the variations that are normally to be expected in language? We know now that all of these variations are manifestations within the over-all system of the language, and that we may choose a standard dialect as actually spoken in everyday communication as a dependable source where we may study the central core of the language. We know from the experience of modern linguistics that this spoken form of a language exemplifies a maximum of its structure in its most direct expression.

In our comparison we will do well to choose a specific dialect of the native language and a specific dialect of the language to be learned, the chief reason for this being that the learner proceeds in that fashion: he goes from a specific dialect of his native language to a specific dialect of the foreign language, usually that of his teacher or teachers, sometimes that of his learning materials. If a cluster of dialects is compared at the same time as representing the language, there is danger that the picture will not be clear for any one dialect. The statements will tend to refer now to this dialect, now to that one, with loss of sharpness in the description of the system of any particular dialect. Important differences in dialects and styles might well be relegated to footnotes.

6. Necessity of Validating the Results of the Theoretical Comparative Analysis.

The list of problems resulting from the comparison of the foreign language with the native language will be a most significant list for teaching, testing, research, and understanding. Yet it must be considered a list of hypothetical problems until final validation is achieved by checking it against the actual speech of students. This final check will show in some instances that a problem was not adequately analyzed and may be more of a problem than predicted. In this kind of validation we must keep in mind of course that not all the speakers of a language will have exactly the same amount of difficulty with each problem. Dialectal and personal differences rule out such a possibility. The problems will nevertheless prove quite stable and predictable for each language background.

7. Sample of Style Used in Presenting a Linguistic Comparison.

Although the value of linguistic comparisons such as we have been describing in this book lies chiefly in their immediate use for teaching materials, tests, etc., the comparisons may be written up for publication or other distribution in order to make the information available to others. The compact outline of the structure of the two languages need not be discussed here. Any consistent outline style will do. The process of comparing the two structures, pattern by pattern, could be presented in regular paragraph form, with a paragraph for a pattern in the native language, a paragraph for the nearest pattern in the foreign language, and a third one for comments on the comparison.

Another style, which I favor at present, has the advantage of easy rechecking and ready comparison. It consists in giving the inventory of the foreign language pattern in the left column of a two-column page, a parallel inventory of the most similar pattern of the native language in the right column at the same level on the page, and the description of problems extending clear across the page under both inventories. Separate descriptions for production and recognition should be given always, even if the recognition problem is identical with the production one. In such cases the description need not be repeated word for word but might simply be stated as "same as production." When there is no problem for recognition or production or both, the description would simply read "None." Following is a sample of presentation:

COMPARISON OF ENGLISH AND SPANISH
QUESTION PATTERNS

ENGLISH	SPANISH
Pattern 1.	
Form: Be $\longleftrightarrow$ he (D 1) [16]	Form: *Ser* (or *estar, tener, hacer*) and intonation signal.
Example: *Is he a farmer?*	Example: *¿Es un campesino?*
Features: (1) Occurrence of *be* before *he*.	Features: (1) Occurrence of *ser* with or without a class 1.
(2) Sentence tie, $\longleftrightarrow$, between *he* and *be*.	(2) Sentence tie between *ser* and subject when expressed.

[16]Symbols are from Fries, *Ibid*. "$\longleftrightarrow$" represents a correlation of forms signaling a sentence tie. D is a determiner, e.g., *the, a, this*, etc. The number 1 represents a class 1 word, e.g., *farmer, student*, etc.

(3) Presence of *he*.	(3) Subject pronoun often omitted.
(4) High-low intonation quite possible with this pattern.	(4) Intonation rise to high or rise to extra high with drop to mid or low.
Meaning: 'question.' Yes-no response type.	Meaning: 'question.' Yes-no response type.
Distribution: Restricted to *be* and *have*.	Distribution: No special restrictions.

Problems of Spanish speaker learning English:
   Production: (1) May not place *be* before *he*.
               (2) May omit subject pronoun.
               (3) Will give a rising intonation, mid—high, or rise to extra high.
               (4) Will use the same pattern with verbs other than *be* and *have*.
   Recognition: (1) Will mistake question for statement because of falling, high—low, intonation in English.

No special problem with meaning.

Chapter 4

HOW TO COMPARE TWO VOCABULARY SYSTEMS

1. Words.

1.1 Undue emphasis on words as words to the neglect of pronunciation and grammatical structure is not in keeping with modern linguistic thinking. Sapir says bluntly in talking about linguistic study, "The linguistic student should never make the mistake of identifying a language with its dictionary."[1] On the other hand, one cannot deny or ignore the existence of the word as a tangible unit of language. Sapir, again with characteristic insight, puts it thus:

> No more convincing test could be desired than this, that the naïve Indian, quite unaccustomed to the concept of the written word, has nevertheless no serious difficulty in dictating a text to a linguistic student word by word; he tends, of course, to run his words together as in actual speech, but if he is called to a halt and is made to understand what is desired, he can readily isolate the words as such, repeating them as units. He regularly refuses, on the other hand, to isolate the radical or grammatical element, on the ground that it "makes no sense."[2]

1.2 The word has been defined for scientific linguistic study by Bloomfield:

> A free form which consists entirely of two or more lesser free forms, as, for instance, *poor John* or *John ran away* or *yes, sir*, is a *phrase*. A free form which is not a phrase, is a *word*. A word, then, is a free form which does not consist entirely of (two or more) lesser free forms; in brief, a word is a *minimum free form*.[3]

1.3 A clear insight into the way words are used by the speakers of a language is given by Fries. He says:

---

[1]Edward Sapir, *Language* (New York: Harcourt, Brace, and Co., 1921), p. 234.
[2]*Ibid.*, pp. 34-35.
[3]Leonard Bloomfield, *Language* (New York: Henry Holt and Co., 1933), p. 178.
For a more complete discussion see also pp. 178-83 and 207-46. For a mechanical procedure that shows word and morpheme boundaries see the recent article by Zellig S. Harris, "From Phoneme to Morpheme," *Language*, XXXI (1955), 190-222.

For us, a *word* is a combination of sounds acting as a stimulus to bring into attention the experience to which it has become attached by use....[4]

More than that, while the experience that is stimulated by the sound combination is a whole with a variety of contacts, usually only one aspect of this experience is dominant in attention — a particular aspect determined by the whole context of the linguistic situation. When one uses *head* in such a context as "a *head* of cabbage," it is the shape which is the dominant aspect of the experience that has made a connection with the material unit, a cabbage. When one uses head in such a context as "the *head* of a department," it is the head as the chief or dominating part of the body. When it is used in "the *head* of the river," another aspect of the relation of head to the body is important in attention. From a practical point of view, the various separate dictionary meanings of a word are the particular aspects of the experience stimulated by a word that have been dominant in the attention of users of the word as these aspects may be inferred from the context of a large number of quotations in which the word appears. For the native user of a language, the symbol, with the wide range of experience it stimulates, is so much a part of the very texture of his thought that he exercises great freedom in turning upon any aspect of this experience in line with the pressing needs of his thinking. The "meanings" of words are, therefore, more fluid than we realize. For the foreign speaker of a language who learns this new language as an adult, the words as stimuli probably never function with anything like the same fullness and freedom as they do for a native.[5]

1.4   Three aspects of words concern us here: (1) their form, (2) their meaning, and (3) their distribution.

1.4.1   *Form.* In most languages the form of words consists of sound segments, stress, and, in tone languages such as Chinese and Thai, pitch. The form of the Spanish word *jugo* 'juice' is the sequence of four significant sound segments (phonemes) /xúgo/ and stress — primary stress on the first syllable. If we change one of the sound segments, for example the one represented by *j* to /y/, a new word results: *yugo* 'yoke.' If we change the position of the primary stress, another word results: *jugó* 'he played.' The Thai word ม้า [ma:ʔ] 'horse' is made up of sound segments and a high, level pitch. The same segments with a rising pitch would mean 'dog.'

The form of words varies according to the formality of the situation, speed of talk, position in the sentence, position as to stress, etc. For example, the English word *and* varies from three segmental phonemes /æ nd/ through intermediate degrees of reduction, /ənd/, /æn/, /ən/, to one segmental phoneme, /n/.

---

[4]Charles C. Fries, with the co-operation of A. Aileen Traver, *English Word Lists, A Study of Their Adaptability for Instruction* (Washington, D. C.: American Council on Education, 1940. Reprinted Ann Arbor: Wahr Publishing Co., 1950), p. 87.

[5]*Ibid.*, p. 88.

The word *not* occurs as /nat/ and /nt/; *will* as /wɪl/ and as /l/; *is* as /ɪz/ and as /s/ or /z/. Native speakers of the language find it difficult to believe that the words they use vary so much in form.

Another relevant feature of form is that of the parts of words. English *observational* is made up of a stem *observ-* (compare *observe*),[6] a suffix *-(a)tion*, and another suffix *-al*. Other languages permit more complex combinations than those of English. As something of a linguistic curiosity, but definitely a form of the language, Sapir mentions the example from Paiute, an American Indian language of southwestern Utah, *wii-to-kuchum-punku-rügani-yugwi-va-ntü-m(ü)*, meaning 'they who are going to sit and cut up with a knife a black cow (or bull).'[7]

The frequency of the parts of words may counterbalance the lack of frequency of the total word. If we use the word *observational,* for example, it will probably be understood by elementary students studying English as a foreign language even though it appears among the 1,358 least frequent words in Thorndike's list.[8] The parts *observ-* + *(a)tion* + *al* are much more frequent than the word itself. *Observ-* as the word *observe* is listed by Thorndike among the 2,000 most frequent words in English. The suffix *-tion* is used in so many words in English that its total frequency must be very high. I found examples of *-tion* in every page of a random ten-page sample of Bloomfield's *Language* and in a similar spot-check of ten random pages of the lighter style of *The Art of Plain Talk* by Rudolf Flesch.[9] The suffix *-al* is less frequent than *-tion,* but it is still frequent enough to occur on practically every page of a text.

English has lexical forms made up of patterns of separate words, for example, *call up* 'to phone.' Many languages do not permit such units or do not permit the same types of formal patterns. Compare for example Spanish *telefonear* 'to telephone' or *llamar for teléfono* 'call by telephone' but nothing like the construction *call up.*

1.4.2 *Meaning.* It is quite an illusion to think, as even literate people sometimes do, that meanings are the same in all languages, that languages differ only in the forms used for those meanings.

---

[6] It is doubtful that native speakers break this form further into *ob* + *serve*.

[7] Sapir, *Language*, p. 31.

[8] Edward L. Thorndike and Irving Lorge, *The Teachers' Word Book of 30,000 Words* (New York: Bureau of Publications, Teachers College, Columbia University, 1944).

[9] New York: Harper & Brothers Publishers, 1946.

As a matter of fact the meanings into which we classify our experience are culturally determined or modified, and they vary considerably from culture to culture. Some meanings found in one culture may not exist in another. The meaning 'horse' did not exist in American Indian languages until the Spanish conquest and colonization brought horses to America. Similarly, the meanings 'corn' (in the sense of maize) and 'potatoes' did not exist in Europe until the same people took those products from America to Europe in their ships. But even when the reality is available to the culture, the meanings will differ, or not exist in some cases. The Eskimos have many meaning distinctions correlating with different types of snow and use separate words to express those distinctions, whereas other cultures that have considerable experience with snow simply do not have as many meaning distinctions. These meaning differences are seldom as forcefully noticeable as when one attempts to translate accurately a text from one language to another.

Meanings can be classified according to the forms to which they attach. Meanings that attach to words as words are lexical meanings, for example, the meaning, 'a building for human habitation,' that attaches to the form *house* is a lexical meaning in English. The meaning 'two or more, plural' that attaches to the bound form -*s* [s] in *books, cats, maps,* can be called a morphological meaning, while the same meaning 'plural' that attaches to the word form *plural* is a lexical meaning. The meaning 'question' attached to the word arrangement in the sentence, *Is he a farmer?* is a syntactic meaning, but the meaning 'question' attached to the word form *question* is a lexical one.

At the moment, we are primarily concerned with lexical meanings, but different languages classify their meanings differently, that is, what is habitually a lexical meaning in one language may be a morphological meaning in another. Speakers of one language who have not come in meaningful contact with other languages assume not only that the meanings are the same but that they will be classified the same way. Speakers of English find it difficult to imagine a language in which the singular-plural distinction in *book : books* is not made morphologically. "How else can you communicate that idea?" they are apt to ask. In Chinese, for example, that distinction is not made, that is, it is not made morphologically, by a bound form such as -*s* in English. In Chinese, the meanings 'two' 'three' 'more than one,' etc., are lexical meanings; those meanings attach to words. When the meaning is relevant to the message, the words are included, and when the meaning is not relevant, the words are left out. Classical

Greek had the meanings 'singular' 'dual' and 'plural' as morphological meanings. We can assume that Greek speakers wondered how languages that had only singular and plural could express the meaning 'dual, two.' That distinction is a lexical one in English.

The frequency of the various meanings of a word is relevant. If we used the word *get,* which appears among the 500 most frequent ones in Thorndike's list, in the context, *We did not want to overdo the thing and get six months,* meaning 'suffer imprisonment by way of punishment,' we would find that some fairly advanced students of English as a foreign language would not 'know' the word. Yet we could not convincingly assume that they did not really know one of the 500 most frequent words in English. That particular meaning of *get* is so infrequent that it was not reported as having occurred at all in a sample of over half a million running words.[10] The *Oxford English Dictionary* lists 234 meanings for the word *get,* and obviously one can know a good many of those meanings and still miss the word in the particular context used above.

The meanings discussed thus far are usually part of the intended message in communication. These meanings are more or less consciously intended by the speaker and may be called primary meanings. In actual use, however, other meanings are conveyed by words; for example, if a word is restricted in use to a given social class, its use by a speaker may give the listener the meaning of social class identification. Similarly if a word is restricted to a geographical area, its use by a speaker may convey a locality meaning also.

1.4.3 The *distribution* of words is important to us because at any given moment in the history of a language the speakers of that language carry with them the habits of the restrictions in distribution, also because different languages have different restrictions. There are grammatical restrictions so that in English, for example, *water* may be a noun as in *a glass of water,* a verb as in *water the garden,* a noun adjunct as in *water meter,* but not an adjective without some previous adjustment in form, e. g., *watery substance.* In other languages the restrictions may be greater; for example in Spanish, *agua* 'water' may only be a noun unless its form is changed.

The fact that words may show different geographic distribution, falling in or out of a dialect area, is important. And, as already

---

[10]Estimated from data supplied in Irving Lorge, *The Semantic Count of 570 Commonest English Words* (New York: Bureau of Publications, Teachers College, Columbia University, 1949).

indicated, distribution in the various social-class levels also has to be considered because of the secondary meanings such distribution conveys. Statements of raw frequency alone leave these matters unresolved. Thorndike's list gives *ain't* among the 2,000 most frequent words in English, but the list does not say if *ain't* is typical of Standard English or of the speech representing certain other dialects.

Words are not only restricted geographically and socially; they are often restricted as to styles of speaking and writing. For example, many words found in poetry will not be found in ordinary conversation or in ordinary prose, and vice versa.

1.5 *Classifications.* It should be abundantly clear now that the words of a language are a highly complex system of classes of items — classes interlocking as to meaning, form, grammatical function, distribution, etc.

1.5.1 Fries classifies English words into four groups that seem relevant to us.[11] They are (1) function words, (2) substitute words, (3) grammatically distributed words, and (4) content words. The function words primarily perform grammatical functions, for example *do* signaling questions. The substitute words *he, she, they, so,* etc. replace a class of words and several subclasses. Grammatically distributed words, *some, any,* etc., show unusual grammatical restrictions in distribution. The number of words in the first three groups is rather small, say approximately 200 in English.[12] The fourth group, content words, constitutes the bulk of the vocabulary of the language. In English and in many other languages the content words are subdivided into items treated as things, as processes, as qualities, etc.

1.5.2 Two further distinctions in vocabulary are required to complete our model. We need to distinguish between a common core vocabulary, known to all the members of a language community, and specialized vocabularies, known only to special groups. We are of course primarily interested in the common core vocabulary, because specialized vocabularies have to be learned by native as well as nonnative speakers. We are interested primarily in the special problems of the latter.

1.5.3 The other distinction is that made between vocabulary for production and vocabulary for recognition. As a rule our recognition vocabulary is much larger than our production

---

[11]Charles C. Fries, *Teaching and Learning English as a Foreign Language* (Ann Arbor: Univ. Mich. Press, 1945), pp. 44-50.

[12]Estimated from data supplied in Charles C. Fries, *The Structure of English* (New York: Harcourt, Brace, and Co., 1952), Chap. VI.

vocabulary. Various estimates have been made of the minimum necessary number of words that will enable a student to communicate in ordinary situations. Basic English uses approximately 1,000 for that purpose.[13] Michael West considers a vocabulary of 2,000 words "enough for anything, and more than enough for most things."[14] Obviously these are minimum production vocabularies. For recognition, larger minimum vocabularies are necessary.

2. The Native Language Factor.

2.1 *Ease and difficulty.* Making use of available vocabulary studies one might attempt to select a sample vocabulary for teaching or for testing. Such attempts have been made and have received wide circulation. C. K. Ogden's *Basic English* list and West's *A General Service List of English Words*[15] are well-known examples in an active field. Nevertheless, in spite of the care and experience that have gone into the preparation of such lists, they cannot give us a vocabulary sample graded as to difficulty because by their very nature they fail to take into account the most powerful factor in acquiring the vocabulary of a foreign language, namely, the vocabulary of the native language.

If, for example, in a test of English vocabulary for Spanish speakers one uses the words *machete, suppuration,* and *calumniator,* which appear among the 1,358 least frequent words in Thorndike's 30,000 word list, one would find that practically all the students knew them. Could we then assume that those students possessed a vocabulary of over 28,642 words in English? Obviously not. Because Spanish has the words *machete, supuración,* and *calumniador,* similar in form and meaning to the English words, Spanish-speaking students will know them. We simply cannot ignore the native language of the student as a factor of primary importance in vocabulary, just as we cannot ignore it in pronunciation and grammatical structure.

Another example arguing for the importance of the native language has to do with grammatical distribution of two very simple words. The words *fire* and *man* will probably be more difficult for Spanish speakers in the contexts, *Fire the furnace,* and *Man*

---

[13]C. K. Ogden, *The System of Basic English* (New York: Harcourt, Brace, and Co., 1934).

[14]"Simplified and Abridged," *English Language Teaching,* V, No. 2, 48.

[15]Michael West, *A General Service List of English Words with Semantic Frequencies and a Supplementary Word-List for the Writing of Popular Science and Technology* (New York, London, Toronto: Longmans, Greene and Co., 1953).

the guns, than in *Open fire* 'start shooting' and *A man broke his leg.* The relationships are more subtle than in the previous example, but are there nevertheless. Spanish has a noun, *fuego,* 'fire' used in *Abran fuego,* 'Open fire' but it is not used as a verb. Similarly, a Spanish noun, *hombre,* 'man,' is used in *Un hombre se rompió una pierna,* 'A man broke his leg,' but is not used as a verb. There are other elements involved in these examples to be sure, but grammatical distribution is definitely a factor.

2.2 *Difficulty patterns.* Similarity to and difference from the native language in form, meaning, and distribution will result in ease or difficulty in acquiring the vocabulary of a foreign language. Comparing the foreign language vocabulary with that of the native language we will find words that are (1) similar in form and in meaning, (2) similar in form but different in meaning, (3) similar in meaning but different in form, (4) different in form and in meaning, (5) different in their type of construction, (6) similar in primary meaning but different in connotation, and (7) similar in meaning but with restrictions in geographical distribution.

Since some of these groups overlap, with the result that some words will fall into more than one group, the difficulty will vary somewhat. Nevertheless, we can predict general level of difficulty on the basis of these groupings, and will classify each group into one of three levels of difficulty: (1) easy, (2) normal, and (3) difficult.

The term *similar* is restricted here to items that would function as "same" in both languages in ordinary use. We know that complete sameness is not to be expected in language behavior. The actual behavioral boundaries of similarity depend on the items that persons of one language "identify" or "translate" as same from and into the other language. References to form are to the sounds of the words, not to the spelling, even though spelling rather than phonetic representation is often used in this chapter.

2.2.1 *Cognates:*[16] Words that are similar in form and in meaning. English and Spanish have thousands of words that are reasonably similar in form and in meaning: *Hotel, hospital,*

---

[16] "Cognates" here are words that are similar in form and meaning regardless of origin. The usual meaning of the term is "related in origin." For us even if two words are not related in origin they will be called cognates if they are similar in form and meaning. Similarly, if two words have the same origin but are now so different that speakers of the two languages do not identify them as similar, they will not be considered cognates for our purposes.

calendar are obvious examples.[17] Some of these cognates survived in Spanish as it evolved from Latin and were borrowed into English from Latin or French. Some go back earlier to forms presumably found in Indo-European, the common ancestor of English and Spanish, which belong to what is known as the Indo-European family of languages. Whatever the cause of the similarity, these words usually constitute the lowest difficulty group — they are easy. In fact, if they are similar enough, even Spanish-speaking students who have never studied English will recognize them. These words are of value at the very elementary level of mastery of the language.

Even though there are thousands of words that are similar in English and Spanish these similarities can be classified into a relatively small number of subgroups or patterns of correspondence, for example, the correspondence between English *-tion* and Spanish *-cion*. Hundreds of words can be classified as similar under that pattern of correspondence.[18] When using such cognate words in teaching and testing we will do well to sample them as patterns rather than as independent items.

It is sometimes falsely assumed that cognates are to be found only between two related languages such as English and Spanish, and not between unrelated languages such as English and Japanese or English and Chinese. In actual fact, numerous cognates can be found between English and Japanese and between English and Chinese, and between many other languages which are quite unrelated to each other. There are many words which have circled the globe, and many more that have extended far beyond the boundaries of any one language or any one culture.

2.2.2 *Deceptive Cognates:*[19] Words that are similar in form but mean different things. Words that are similar in form in two languages may be partly similar in meaning; they may be altogether different in meaning but represent meanings that exist in the native language; or they may be different in meaning and

---

[17]For a list of Spanish-English cognates see Marshall E. Nunn and Herbert A. Van Scroy, *Glossary of Related Spanish-English Words* (Univ. Ala.: University of Alabama Studies, Number 5, 1949).

[18]For a brief account of nine patterns of Spanish-English cognates see *Lessons in Vocabulary* in *An Intensive Course in English,* research staff of the English Language Institute, Charles C. Fries, Director (Ann Arbor: English Language Institute, 1954). See also E. M. Anthony, "The Teaching of Cognates," *Language Learning,* IV (1952-53), 79-82.

[19]"Deceptive cognates" as used here refers only to similarity in form and difference in meaning; it does not refer to the origin of the words. In usual linguistic terminology deceptive cognates would refer to words in two languages that because of their form would seem to be related by origin but are not so related. For us such a case would be classed as a cognate provided the meanings were also similar.

represent meanings which have no basis in experience for someone going from the native language into the foreign one. Japanese
borrowed the word *milk* from English but restricted it, for a time
at least, to 'canned milk.' The form of the word in Japanese is
similar to the English word but the meaning is only partly similar
since it does not include fresh milk, for example. Spanish has a
word, *asistir,* which is similar in form to English *assist,* but the
meaning is practically always different. Spanish *asistir* is similar in meaning to English *attend,* while English *assist* carries
with it the feature of helping, of supporting. As a result of this
difference in meaning, Spanish speakers learning English say
they *assisted a class* when meaning that they *attended* 'were
present.' English *in the table* and *on the table* are expressed in
Spanish as *en la mesa* in ordinary conversation. Only under very
special circumstances will a Spanish speaker make a meaning
distinction between *in* and *on* the table, and then it will not be only
an *in : on* contrast but a *table* versus *drawer* contrast as well.
Spanish speakers will say *en el cajón* 'in the drawer' and *sobre
la mesa* 'on the table.' The problem here is not simply attaching
a familiar meaning to a new form but also grasping a new meaning distinction, a different way of classifying reality.

These words that are similar in form but different in meaning
— deceptive cognates, as we have called them — constitute a special group very high on a scale of difficulty. We will label them
difficult. They are not adequately sampled on frequency criteria
alone because their similarity in form to words in the native
language raises their frequency in student usage above that normal for the language. In other words, they are more important
than their frequency rating might indicate. They are sure-fire
traps.

2.2.3 *Different forms:* Words that are the "same" in a particular meaning but different in form. Difficulty level: normal.
Example, English *tree* in the context, *The leaves of that tree are
falling,* and Spanish *arbol* in a comparable context. The learning
burden in this case is chiefly that of learning a new form, *tree,*
or *arbol,* for a meaning already habitually grasped in the native
language. This kind of vocabulary learning is naively taken by
many to represent all vocabulary learning. Such an oversimplification fails to account for the great range in difficulty that one
actually finds in learning the vocabulary of a foreign language.

It is also important to note that although certain meanings of
a word in one language are sometimes translatable into a word in
another language there are very few if any words in two languages

that are the same in all their meanings. It is difficult for example
to realize that the words *tree* and *arbol* are similar in only four
out of their twenty or more meanings and uses. Only the poorest
two-language dictionaries will show words on a one-to-one meaning correspondence in the two languages. Only words such as
penicillin, which are borrowed into many languages simultane-
ously, can be considered equivalent in all their meanings, and
even then if such words gain any currency at all they soon develop
new meanings that are not parallel in different languages.

It is in these content words that are different in form but
similar in some meanings, however, that decisions can and should
be made as to vocabulary size. These decisions can be made
partly on the basis of frequency lists for recognition vocabulary,
and also on the range of usefulness in a production vocabulary.

2.2.4 *"Strange" Meanings:* Words that are different in form
and represent meanings that are "strange" to speakers of a particular native language, that is, meanings that represent a different grasp of reality, are classified as difficult. In American
English, *first floor* is different in form from Spanish *primer piso*
and different in its grasp of what constitutes 'first.' Spanish
primer 'first' in this case does not mean number one at ground
level but number one above ground level, and so *primer piso* refers to what in American English is called *second floor,* although
first floor would be its literal translation.

These cases constitute special problems in the vocabulary of
a foreign language. Obviously it is not enough merely to teach a
new form: the strange meaning must be made familiar also.
Some of these words with "strange" meanings may happen to be
similar in form in the two languages. They are then deceptive
cognates as well. The partial overlap of the two groups does not
reduce the need to identify them separately. When words fall in
both groups their learning difficulty increases accordingly.

There is every reason to believe that the same kind of distortion that we can observe in the sounds of the speech of a nonnative
speaker also occurs in the meanings he is trying to convey. In
both cases he is substituting the units and patterns of his native
language and culture. In the case of sound the untrained person
who listens to him hears a vague "foreign" accent and the trained
person hears specific distortions. In the case of meanings the
distortions go largely undetected because the meanings intended
by the speaker are not directly observable by the listener. It is
only when a word form is used in an "unusual" way that our attention is drawn to possible meaning differences. Similarly, when

the nonnative speaker of a language listens to the language as spoken by natives, the meanings that he grasps are not those that the native speakers attempt to convey, but those of the system of the language of the listener.

2.2.5 *New Form Types:* Words that are different in their morphological construction. Difficult. When the speakers of various Romance languages or of Japanese, Chinese, and other languages learn English they have great trouble learning such lexical items as *call up* 'to telephone,' *call on* 'to visit,' and *run out of* 'to exhaust the supply of.' If in the native language of the student there are no lexical items made up of two otherwise separate words in patterns like the one illustrated, he will not easily grasp these "two-word verbs" in the foreign language. The difficulty is increased when the elements can be separated by other words, as in the example *Did you call the boy up?* These two-word verbs constitute a difficulty group all its own.

"Idioms" — expressions peculiar to a language — are identifiable as we compare two languages rather than within a language itself. An expression which may seem to a native speaker to belong exclusively to his language may be quite natural to speakers of another language and would therefore not be an "idiom" to them. On the other hand, an expression which seems quite natural to native speakers may be strange to foreign speakers of a particular language background. If we should find on comparing an expression in a variety of languages that it is strange to all or nearly all of them, we would be justified in calling it an idiom in general, but even then the statement would be meaningless in those cases in which another language had a parallel expression. As a matter of fact, the idiom counts made in the wake of the Modern Foreign Language Study were two-language studies. The *Spanish Idiom List* by Keniston[20] gives expressions in Spanish that are strange to English speakers. In all of the counts the compilers looked at expressions in the foreign language with English as their frame of reference, whether they realized it or not.

2.2.6 *Different Connotation:* Words that have widely different connotations in two languages. Difficult. A special difficulty group is represented by words that are harmless in connotation in the native language but offensive or taboo in the foreign language, or vice versa. When they are harmless in the native

---

[20]Hayward Keniston, *Spanish Idiom List Selected on the Basis of Range and Frequency of Occurrence,* Publications of the American and Canadian Committees on Modern Languages, XI (New York, 1929).

language the student will use them in the foreign language without
realizing their effect. Even when they are harmless in the foreign language the student will avoid using them for fear of setting
off the same reactions they produce in his native language. In
either case they are important on the level of social acceptability
of words. A few examples will show how important these connotation differences can be.

In Spanish the expression *Dios mío,* meaning literally 'My
God,' is often used as an appeal to the Almighty in matter-of-fact
conversation. Even those Spanish speakers who have progressed
considerably in their control of English will sometimes use the
expression with the same feeling and intent in English, but the
effect on English listeners is of course different. The name *Jesús*
is often used as a given name in Spanish. Parents who thus name
their children may actually feel they are honoring Christ, or at
least they do not feel any lack of respect. In English, however,
people find it difficult to call a person by that name. It seems to
smack of irreverence to English speakers to use the name for a
human being, a radically different connotation from that in Spanish. Whistling at sports events or political rallies shows a difference in the opposite direction. Spanish speakers may be
shocked to hear a speaker whistled at and applauded at the same
time. To them applause indicates approval, and whistling, a
vulgar form of disapproval.

These differences in connotation sometimes develop between
dialects of the same language. In Cuba the familiar form of the
second person pronoun, *tú*, is more widely used than in Mexico,
for example. A Cuban young man was rebuked by two Mexican
young ladies because he used the familiar *tú,* which sounded a bit
too bold to them. No amount of explaining was enough to completely convince the girls that the young man actually meant no
disrespect. The word *grueso* 'fat' is used as a compliment at
least in some dialects of present-day Spanish. On a visit to Spain
I was greeted repeatedly with "flattering" expressions of how
"fat" I was. Being aware of the favorable connotation I had to
appreciate the remark.

These have been obvious and sometimes coarse examples of
wide differences in connotation. More subtle differences exist
and remain with speakers of a foreign language even through the
advanced stages of control of the language. We cannot do much
to teach or to test these subtle differences specifically and completely, but it is possible to sample the more frequent and obvious cases of wide discrepancy in connotation.

2.2.7 *Geographical Restrictions:* Words that are restricted to certain geographic areas within the area of the foreign language. Difficult, because the restrictions must be learned also. Restrictions in geographic distribution of words are important to the selection of words for teaching and for testing. Unless we are interested in teaching or testing a particular geographic dialect of a language we will choose forms that are part of the standard language, if there is one, or words that are common to the major dialects if there is not a standard language. If we are interested in English without regard to whether it is Standard British or Standard American English we would avoid such words as *petrol* and *gasoline* in testing because they are typical of British and American usage respectively. If, on the other hand, we are interested in Standard American English as distinct from British English, we would use *gasoline*. Within American English, if we are not interested in any one dialect, we would use *dragon fly* for the insect known by that name, because that term is more general than Northern *darning needle* and Midland *snake feeder,* other names for the same insect.[21]

Although part of what has been said about geographically restricted words may not apply directly to the definition of a pattern of difficulty, we are justified in considering such words a special difficulty group, because a student who has learned a restricted form must learn another for the same meaning if he is to communicate with speakers from geographic areas where the form he learned has no currency. Hence, the label, difficult, we have given them.

There has been on the whole much superficial oversimplified thinking about the vocabulary of languages, and a great deal of vocabulary research, such as that of word frequency counts and simplified vocabularies, often suffers from that deficiency. In dealing with vocabulary we should take into account three important aspects of words — their form, their meaning, their distribution — and we should consider the various kinds or classes of words in the operation of the language. These things are particularly important when one learns the vocabulary of a foreign language since the forms, meanings, distribution, and classifications of words are different in different languages. Out of these differences arise vocabulary problems and difficulty levels that constitute teaching and learning problems and are telltale matters

---

[21]Hans Kurath, *A Word Geography of the Eastern United States* (Ann Arbor: Univ. Mich. Press, 1949), p. 14.

for vocabulary tests. The patterns of difficulty described above are an attempt to clarify and classify the problems involved.

3. How to Compare Two Vocabularies.

3.1 With the above classification of vocabulary problems in mind we will now attempt to give specific suggestions on how to proceed in a particular case.

3.2 *A limited vocabulary.* The full vocabulary of any of the major languages known is extremely large and would require a lifetime of research to compare, item by item, with any other full vocabulary. Since we are interested in foreign language teaching, testing, research and understanding, however, we can limit the size of the vocabulary to something less than the entire vocabulary range of a language.

The particular way to limit a vocabulary will depend on whether it is a vocabulary for speaking or for listening, for adults or for children, and for any of a variety of purposes and special uses.

The limitation will not have much effect in some types of words. Fries says, "In the matter of vocabulary items this [first] stage of learning must include the chief items (nearly all, in fact) of the first three kinds — 'function' words, 'substitute' words, and words with 'negative and affirmative distribution.' All word lists agree upon the inclusion of the chief items of these three groups, whether the lists were built upon frequency counts or upon some logical principle of selection. These words play a large part in the structural operation of English and must, there-fore, not only be included in any minimum list of vocabulary items to be learned but also be part of the lessons which consti-tute the first stage of that learning process."[22]

Beyond these three categories, the more specific we can be about our purpose in selecting a vocabulary the better defined our limited vocabulary can be. If we can decide that we are interested in a speaking vocabulary: (1) We might then decide to stay roughly within 2,000 words or even within 1,000 words, or we may decide to include more than 2,000 — say 4,000 or even as many as 7,000, depending on the level of mastery expected.

(2) We must decide what meanings of these words we will in-clude within that vocabulary. (3) We should decide what contextual areas will be our concern, in order to include words needed in

---

[22] Fries, *Teaching and Learning English as a Foreign Language,* p. 50.

those areas and eliminate those not needed. (4) We must decide
what grammatical patterns will be included within the range of
our sample. The selection of these grammatical patterns will
decide what function words and what uses of those function words
we will need. These grammatical patterns will also decide what
substitute words and what grammatically distributed words we
will include in our vocabulary. And (5) we should decide what
age groups our vocabulary is intended for so that we may further
choose among vocabulary items that show age distribution.

The actual vocabulary selected will still vary, and no one-shot
solution can be given here. But let's say that we now have our
vocabulary of 2,000 words with the meanings that are relevant to
us. We then proceed to compare that vocabulary with that of the
native language.

3.3 *Specific suggestions on comparing vocabularies.* For
each foreign language word (later for groups or patterns of words
as well) we need to compare form, meaning, distribution, and
connotation with the vocabulary of the native language. This
comparison can either be done using all four tests at once for
each word in the foreign language, or it can be done for the entire
sample, first as to form, then as to meaning, third as to distribution, and finally as to connotation. I do not see any particular
reason to do the comparison one way or another. I proceed by
comparing the entire sample for form first, then meaning, then
distribution, and finally connotation.

First step: comparison of form. Since we assume that the
person making the comparison knows both the foreign and the
native languages well, he can go through his vocabulary sample
in the foreign language, reading aloud each word, and deciding
fairly quickly whether it resembles a native language word or
not. Each word that resembles a native language word has to be
either set aside, if it is on a separate card, or copied on a separate sheet or card. As patterns of similarity become apparent,
these similar words can be further classified into groups.

We will end up with two kinds of words, (1) those that are
different in form, and (2) those that are similar in form. Those
that are similar will be further classified into several patterns
of correspondence between the native and the foreign languages.

Those that are different in form should be looked over once
more to see if they differ not only in form but in the type of construction as well. Those that differ as to type of construction
come under new form types. Going through the list once will not
be enough. We must go back and see if any words that are

similar have been overlooked and to recheck the groups of those that are similar. This rechecking is particularly important because the border between what is similar and what is different is admittedly a fuzzy one, and we must expect some discrepancy if two investigators classify the words without consulting each other. Almost perfect agreement may be reached if two investigators work together.

Second step: comparing meaning. We can then take the words that show similarity in form and check the meanings selected in our list against the meanings of the similar words in the native language. If the meanings are reasonably similar — they seldom if ever coincide exactly — we consider those words as cognates. If the meanings are clearly different, we class the words as deceptive cognates and consider them very difficult.

Next we take the words that are not similar in form to words in the native language. If we find that their meanings are reasonably similar to the meanings of words in the native language we class them as different forms. If the meanings are not similar to meanings in the native language, we class the words under strange meanings. We also class them as strange meanings if the meaning in the foreign language represents only a part of a native language meaning. In other words, there is a meaning problem when the learner has to make a distinction not required in his native language or made differently there.

Third step: comparing distribution and connotation. A final inspection of the list should be made to find words that show wide differences in distribution and/or connotation. Words that may not be used as verbs in the foreign language will constitute problems if they can be so used in the native language. Words that are restricted in geographic distribution in the foreign language will be listed as problems. And finally, words that show wide differences in connotation will constitute problems.

4. Expanding the Vocabulary from a Compared Sample.

From the comparison of a limited vocabulary such as that summarized above we will discover patterns of similarity and difference between the two languages that will apply to vocabulary beyond our sample. Patterns of correspondence in form, with similar meaning, will apply to other words not included in the sample. For teaching purposes those additional words may be brought in without limit as to number. They do not constitute a learning problem because in any attempt to enlarge the vocabulary beyond the sample, the problems will have been set up already.

Problems caused by differences in meanings may be used as
hints to detect similar problems in the added vocabulary, and the
same may be the case with differences in connotation and geographic and other distribution.

5. How to Present the Results of Vocabulary Comparison.

The type of presentation of the results of our comparison will
vary greatly according to the intended use. If the results are to
be used for language learning lessons, they might be presented
by lessons. In such a case there would be a sequence of words
brought in as needed for the grammatical patterns presented,
and other groups of items according to the contextual areas of
each lesson. On the vocabulary for each lesson there would have
to be difficulty-grouping within the patterns described. A general
survey of cognates might be desirable even in a lesson arrangement, however.

If areas and sequence of presentation are not to be shown in
the results, the materials might be classified simply by patterns
of difficulty. This arrangement might be useful in the preparation
of tests. Other arrangements are possible, of course. An alpha-
betical listing of the entire vocabulary sample as in a dictionary,
with summary description of problems involved for each item,
perhaps even in a coded or semi-coded, abbreviated form, might
be convenient for reference purposes.

Chapter 5

HOW TO COMPARE TWO WRITING SYSTEMS

1. Introduction.

1.1 *Learning a writing system is not the same as learning a language.* Bloomfield separates writing systems and language rather vigorously as follows:

> Writing is not language, but merely a way of recording language by means of visible marks. In some countries, such as China, Egypt, and Mesopotamia, writing was practised thousands of years ago, but to most of the languages that are spoken today it has been applied either in relatively recent times or not at all. Moreover, until the days of printing, literacy was confined to a very few people. All languages were spoken through nearly all of their history by people who did not read or write; the languages of such peoples are just as stable, regular, and rich as the languages of literate nations. A language is the same no matter what system of writing may be used to record it, just as a person is the same no matter how you take his picture. The Japanese have three systems of writing and are developing a fourth. When the Turks, in 1928, adopted the Latin alphabet in place of the Arabic, they went on talking in just the same way as before. In order to study writing, we must know something about language, but the reverse is not true.[1]

Everyone has observed that a child learns to speak his native language before he learns to read and write it. It would not make sense to teach a child to write first. He would be reduced to copying meaningless lines, and that is not writing. Writing implies visible symbols that represent language.

The clear separation between language and writing in the learning process of our native language is usually forgotten when teaching or learning a foreign language. The usual mistake consists in beginning the study of a foreign language through its writing system. And actually, the writing process constitutes a problem of its own, distinct from that of learning the foreign language.

The mistake seems to be further encouraged when there is similarity in the writing systems of the two languages. In English, Spanish, French, Italian, and the other languages that use the

---

[1]Leonard Bloomfield, *Language* (New York: Henry Holt and Co., 1933), p. 21.

Latin alphabet, it is possible to transfer many of one's reading habits from the native language to the foreign one — however strange the result may be — and teachers and students fall into this false introduction to the foreign language with great confidence.

In learning a language such as Chinese, which does not use letters in its writing system, the temptation is less strong, and we are more disposed to admit that learning to read and write Chinese is a different problem from learning the Chinese language.

1.2 *The written symbols of each language form a system.* Even in learning to write one's native language it is essential to remember that the symbols used in writing have no absolute value per se but are significant as one part of the system of writing. One does not learn a writing system effectively if he takes the symbols as a collection of unrelated items to be memorized. There is first the type of relation between the symbols and the language units they represent, and there are the distinctive features of the symbols themselves. About the relation between symbols and language we will talk later. Suffice it to say here that in languages in which the letters of the alphabet represent reasonably well the phonemes of the language a systematic approach to the study of writing is easy to justify and to accept. In other languages, such as English for example, in which the correspondence between sounds and writing is more complex, it is surprising how often the idea of learning the writing as a collection of items is entertained. Yet even in English there is sufficient patterning of spelling representation to warrant a system approach rather than a word item approach such as that observed in many schools. It is more of a burden to learn each word as if it were a totally new writing unit than to learn spelling in patterns of words which show uniform representation of the sounds of English.

And it is interesting to note that even in Chinese writing, called sometimes logographic because it represents words (or morphemes) instead of phonemes, each written character is not entirely different from every other character, but contains parts that are found systematically in other characters. We are told that "The compound symbols of Chinese writing can all be analysed into 214 constituents ('radicals')."[2]

One result of the fact that the written symbols of a language

---

[2] *Ibid.*, p. 286.

form a system is that not all the features of the symbols are
equally important. It is rather painful to have to copy something
written in an unfamiliar alphabet, because we have to copy everything slavishly, not knowing just what features are important.
Copying something in our own alphabet, say English, is much
easier and faster, because we do not have to imitate every symbol
exactly but use the features which we know are important. Take
the letter e for example. Lower case handwritten e to us is a
loop made with a counter clock wise movement, and a lower horn.
A person who has never written the Latin alphabet before will
wonder if the slant of the letter is important, if the size and
shape of the loop, the size of the lower horn, etc., are important.
And not knowing the answers, he will painstakingly try to repro-
duce the model exactly. Actually, the loop is important: if we
have two e's without loops they would look like a u. The horn is
important, for without it the e would look like a curled ending of
a preceding letter but not a letter in itself. The connection with
a following letter is not important, but the open end of the horn is
important to distinguish e from possibly o. In a printed capital
E, the three horizontal lines are important. If we eliminate the
bottom one we have F; if we eliminate the top two we have L; if
we eliminate all three we have I. The length of the middle line is
not significant.

1.3 *Types of writing systems.* It is valuable to know that the
writing systems of the world can be classified into three main
types according to the units of language that they represent.

The first type is that of alphabetic writing. The symbols in
this type of writing represent phonemes of the language — with
greater or less perfection. Most of the written languages of the
world today are of this type, even though historically it was the
latest type to be invented. English, Spanish, French, German,
and many other widely used languages have alphabetic writing
systems. It is generally assumed that alphabetic writing evolved
from Egyptian hieroglyphics, through Phoenician writing, which
represented the consonants only, to Greek writing, which represented for the first time consonants and vowels. Among the well
known alphabets of the world are the Latin alphabet, the Arabic
alphabet, the Cyrillic alphabet, and the Greek alphabet. Together
they account for many of the writing systems of the world.

The second type is that of syllabic writing. The symbols represent syllables rather than phonemes. A good many languages
have syllabaries as their writing systems. Cherokee, an American Indian language, is sometimes used as an example of a

language with a syllabic writing system. In this particular case
we happen to know the name of the person who invented the system and the approximate date when it was made known: the Indian
chief Sequoya in 1821. The most widely known language using a
syllabic system of writing is Japanese, which uses a combination
of logographic and syllabic writing. The stems of words are
written with Chinese characters, which are called *Kanji*. Other
elements of the language are represented by means of a syllabary.
Actually, two sets of written syllabic symbols are used, the *Kata-
kana* and *Hiragana*.

The third type is that of logographic writing. The symbols
represent words (or morphemes) rather than phonemes or syllables. The classical example is Chinese. The characters of
Chinese writing may represent quite different-sounding words in
the various so-called dialects of Chinese, but they represent
specific words with form and meaning. Because the meaning
may be the same in two languages, Chinese and Japanese, for
example, the characters constitute a sort of international written
language. That aspect, however, is not our primary concern at
this time.

1.4 *Regularity of fit.* Ideally a writing system should have a
one-to-one relation between its symbols and the language units
they represent. That is, an alphabetic system should have one
letter for each phoneme of the language, and no more. And each
symbol should always represent the same phoneme. Similarly,
in syllabic writing or logographic writing there should be one
symbol for each distinct syllable or word, no more and no less.
In actual fact, except for some theoretical writing system devised
scientifically and used scientifically, we never find that ideal
situation in any of the writing systems in use. A symbol may
represent various phonemes, the same phoneme may be represented by various symbols; sometimes there are more symbols
than phonemes, other times there are more phonemes than symbols, etc. The more regular the fit, the easier it is to learn the
writing system once we know the language. English writing is
particularly bad as to regularity of fit. Turkish, Spanish, Finnish,
and others are better in this respect.

1.5 *Knowing how to read and write involves habits.* Anyone
who masters the writing system of his native language has of
necessity established sets of habits which involve automatic association between the symbols and the language units they represent and the skill for rapid writing (not drawing) of the symbols.
Because these associations and skills are learned fairly early in

life and because they have become subconscious habits, we forget
the great effort involved in learning them. We are surprised,
however, to see an Arab write Arabic script with great speed and
dexterity from right to left on the page. We are quite unable to
write English with any speed from right to left. If you try it, and
I suggest that you do, you will write very slowly, you will make
many errors, and your writing will look very childish in style.
Our surprise is even greater when we see a Japanese or Chinese
writing Chinese characters with great speed and seeming ease.
Their achievement is equally dependent on sets of habits.

1.6 *Transfer of native writing habits affects our learning of
the writing system of a foreign language.* No one can doubt that
we tend to transfer our writing habits to a foreign language. We
are less clear on how this transfer will affect our learning of a
foreign language writing system. Obviously, if both languages
use the same symbols, say the letters of the Latin alphabet, the
problems of learning to write and to identify the symbols is automatically eliminated. The only remaining problems will be those
of associating familiar symbols to strange sounds. Such is the
case of English and Spanish, for example. We assume, of course,
that the strange sounds will have been learned as a separate
problem beforehand.

If the two languages use different symbols, but some of the
symbols show some resemblance across languages, part of the
trouble will be in learning new symbols and part in getting ac-
customed to new associations for symbols that are similar to
those of the native language. Such is the case of Russian and
English. In the case of Latin and Arabic writing, the resemblances between symbols may be considered altogether nil, except for the fact that they all represent sounds.

In the case of Chinese and alphabetic languages, the differences are so fundamental that hardly any transfer at all may be
expected to occur, except for the great abstraction involved in
understanding a live language from ink marks on a piece of paper.

1.7 *Need for systematic comparison of systems.* It is not
enough to make a broad comment on differences between writing
systems if we wish to know specifically what the learning problems will be. It would actually be very difficult to discover all
the problems of learning to read and write a foreign language
even by observing a large number of students over a long period
of time. We would overlook some difficulties and misinterpret
others. Only a thorough structural comparison will yield really
useful data on learning problems. And we can actually save time

and have a better chance to achieve completeness by comparing
the two systems beforehand.

2. How to Compare Two Writing Systems.

2.1 *Analyses of Both Systems.* Our approach requires the
analysis of each of the writing systems and then a comparison of
the two. The kind of analysis that we need must contain the
written symbols and the language sounds or other units which the
symbols represent. It must contain the variations of the symbols
and the direction of the lines of writing and reading. An ideal
analysis should contain also the distinctive features of the written
symbols.

2.2 *Comparing two systems that use the same alphabet.* If
the two writing systems use the same alphabet, as for example
English and Spanish, we could proceed as follows:

Step 1: Comparing the symbols.
   (a) *General comparison.*

Spanish:	English:
a, b, c, ch, d, e, f, g, h, i, j, k,	a, b, c, d, e, f, g, h, i, j, k, l,
l, m, n, ñ, o, p, q, r, rr, s, t,	m, n, o, p, q, r, s, t, u, v, w, x,
u, v, w, x, y, z.	y, z.
¿ ? ¡ ! , . ; : - — ·· ´ ( )« »	? ! , . ; : - — ·· ( ) " "
1, 2, 3, 4, 5, 6, 7, 8, 9, 0.	1, 2, 3, 4, 5, 6, 7, 8, 9, 0.
Capitals, italics, bold face, etc.	Capitals, italics, bold face, etc.
Direction: From left to right.	Direction: From left to right.

Since Spanish and English both use the Latin alphabet there will
be no difficulty involved in writing the letters and symbols or in
identifying them.

(b) *Foreign language symbols not found in the native language.*
In spite of the almost complete similarity, we do notice that
Spanish uses ñ, ¿ , ¡ , and ´ which are not used in English. These
will have to be learned by an English writer learning to write
Spanish. The problem, however, is an insignificant one, because
the new symbols can so easily be characterized as an n with a
tilde ˜, an upside-down question mark and exclamation point, and
an accent mark, the latter being the only symbol not easily re-
latable to previous experience.

(c) *Different styles in the written symbols.* In printing, the
styles are pretty much the same in English and Spanish. In handwritten copy, however, English writing today is of many styles

but quite often a slanting type. Spanish-style writing is often of a vertical type. The difference causes no difficulty, however. There are other differences in the symbols that do cause trouble. The English number 7 has no horizontal line as Spanish 7. The Spanish writer unfailingly crosses his 7's in English and the result is interpreted by English readers as the letter *F*.

Spanish number 1 has a fairly long slanting stroke at the top: *1*. English 1 has only the vertical stroke. Writing problem: The Spanish speaker invariably writes his 1 with the slanting stroke at the top, and to the English reader it becomes a 7. Reading problem: None in reading English 1, but in reading handwritten English 7 the Spanish speaker will often interpret it as 1.

(d) *Different distribution of symbols*. Another minor problem is seen in the different distribution of the question mark and exclamation point. In English these marks are used only at the end of the utterance, not at the beginning. In Spanish they appear both at the beginning and at the end.

Writing problem: The Spanish speaker will feel a compulsion to write a question mark or an exclamation point at the beginning of the utterance. The problem, however, is negligible because the speed at which we write is relatively slow, and the habit is easily controlled. Also, it is relatively easy to omit something in the shift to a foreign language.

Reading problem: The Spanish reader will often go through a good part of an English question before realizing that it is a question, and the same is true with exclamations. The absence of a question mark or exclamation point automatically means to him that the sentence is not a question or exclamation.

Step 2: Comparing two writing systems as to relation between sounds and written symbols.

(a) *General*. Continuing with examples from English and Spanish as our illustration, we find the following:

Sample Spanish sounds and their representation:			Sample English sounds and their representation:		
Vowels:			Vowels:		
Pho-nemes[3]	Symbols: letters	Examples	Pho-nemes	Symbols: letters	Examples
/i/	i,y	piso, y	/i/	e,ee,ea, ei,eo,	be,fee,sea,re-ceive,people,

---

[3] In the appendix (p. 123) is a Table of Phonetic and Phonemic Symbols to refer to sounds.

/e/	e	peso		ey,i,ie,	key,machine,belief,
/a/	a	paso		ae,ay,oe.	formulae,quay,poe-
					nology.
/o/	o	poso	/ɪ/	i,y,ie,e,	fit,system,sieve,
/u/	u	puso		ee,o,u,	English,deer,women,
				ui.	business,building.

	Consonants:				Consonants:
/p/	p	pasa	/p/	p,pp.	up, upper.
/t/	t	tasa	/t/	t,tt,ed,	tea,sitting,walked,
				ght,th,tw.	bright,Thomas,two.
/k/	c,qu,k	casa,	/k/	k,ck,c,	key,back,cut,hiccup,
		queso,		cc,cch,	saccharine,chemist,
		kilo.		ch,cq,	acquisition,sacque,
				cque,qu,	liquor,hough.
				gh.	

In Spanish we note a fairly consistent representation of phonemes by letters of the Latin alphabet. A few exceptions can be found easily enough. Note for example h, which is silent; v and b, which represent the same phoneme; y, which sometimes represents the vowel /i/ and sometimes the semi-vowel /y/; c, which may represent /k/ or /θ/in Castilian; and the phoneme /k/, which may be represented by c, qu, or k. Most of these seeming inconsistencies, however, are quite predictable. C, for example, consistently represents /k/ before a, o, u. Before e, i, qu is used to represent /k/. The k spelling is restricted to a few words related to units of the metric system.

In English we are struck by the many minor patterns of representation of the vowels in particular. The relation between sounds and letters is quite complex. Representation of consonants is only slightly less complex than that of the vowels. The tendency to keep the original spelling of each word regardless of origin complicates the writing system tremendously. As a matter of fact, the inconsistencies in present-day English spelling are so numerous that even educated native speakers have to make use of a dictionary quite often when they write something not in ordinary routine prose, and children have to spend an inordinate amount of time and effort to learn the minor spelling patterns.

The picture is not as chaotic, however, as to justify the extreme position that spelling must be learned by sheer memory of each individual word. Many of the spellings are restricted to a few words, and those have to be learned individually, but others form patterns that are better learned as patterns.

Examples: e appears representing both /i/ and /ɪ/, yet it rarely represents /ɪ/. It is more frequent representing /i/ after a consonant: we, he, me, be, she. The letter i appears to represent /i/ and /ɪ/ but it is rare representing /i/. It is quite frequent representing /ɪ/ between consonants: pin, tin, kin, bin, din, chin, shin, etc. ee represents /i/ and /ɪ/ but it is rare representing /ɪ/ and quite frequent for /i/: tee, fee, see, gee, bee, etc.[4]

We can expect an enormous amount of difficulty for a Spanish speaker learning to read and write English. Over and over again he will be misled by spelling, and he will misspell words for a long time. He not only has learned to associate certain sounds with certain symbols, but he has learned to depend on the fairly regular association of letters and sounds in Spanish. The English speaker learning Spanish has less trouble because he goes from a complex system to a fairly simple one.

(b) *Symbols that represent different sounds in the two languages.* A large number of problems appear as we compare the letters and the sounds they represent in English and Spanish. Since we know that the student transfers the habits from his native language to the foreign one, he will have difficulty both in reading and in writing the foreign language whenever a symbol the same as one in his own language represents a different sound in the foreign language. We will describe a few cases by way of illustration.

In English the letter h represents a voiceless velar glide as in *head, hat, hill,* etc. In Spanish the letter h alone represents no sound; it is "silent." The nearest Spanish sound to English /h/ is /x/ as in *jamás, jota, jaca,* etc. Spanish /x/ is a voiceless velar fricative.

Problems for the Spanish speaker learning English:

Writing problem: In trying to write the English sound /h/ a

---

[4] For a discussion of English spelling see Sir William Craigie, *English Spelling, Its Rules and Reasons* (New York: F. S. Crofts & Co., 1927).

Spanish speaker may use the letter j. He may write *hay fever* as
**jey fiver*.

Reading problem: In trying to read English words with the
letter h, a Spanish speaker may interpret it as a silent letter.

Problem for the English speaker learning Spanish:

Writing problem: He will write, or tend to write, Spanish /x/
with the letter h rather than with j. *Jamás* may thus be written
**hamas*.

Reading problem: He definitely attempts to pronounce j with
the sound value it has in English, /ǰ/. The Spanish name *Jiménez*
is pronounced */ǰímɪnɪz/, for example.

English u between consonants often represents the English
mid central vowel /ə/ as in *but, run, cup*. Spanish u, on the other
hand, represents a high back rounded vowel similar to both English /u/ as in *boot* and /ʊ/ as in *foot*.

Problem for the Spanish speaker learning English:

Writing problem: In trying to write the English sound /ə/ the
Spanish speaker will not easily think of the letter u. He may attempt to use o or a. Instead of *hut* he may write *hot* or *hat*.

Reading problem: In attempting to read English u he will
often interpret it as the sound /ʊ/ or /u/. Example: *but* may be
read and understood as *boot*.

Problem for the English speaker learning Spanish:

Writing problem: The English speaker may attempt to write
the Spanish sound /u/ with the frequent English spelling oo.
Thus, theoretically at least, Spanish *agudo* might be written
**agoodo*.

Reading problem: The English speaker will tend to read
Spanish u between consonants as English /ə/.

English i between consonants often represents the sound /ɪ/
as in *fin*. Between consonants but followed by final e it often
represents the diphthong /aɪ/ as in *fine*. Spanish i represents
sounds similar to /ɪ/ and to /i/.

Problem for the Spanish speaker learning English:

Writing problem: In writing the phoneme /ɪ/ or /i/ the Spanish speaker will tend to use i, and in attempting to write the diphthong /aɪ/ he will use ai. Example: *fin* would be written without
difficulty, but *fine* would be attempted as **fain*.

Reading problem: In attempting to read English he will interpret and pronounce *fine* with /i/ or /ɪ/. When corrected a few
times and told that *fine* is pronounced /faɪn/, he will become
confused, and upon finding a word such as *since* he may pronounce
it */saɪns/.

Problem for the English speaker learning Spanish:

Writing problem: In trying to write the sound /i/ the English speaker will attempt to use one of the common English spellings; ee, for example. Spanish *vine* may be rendered **veene*. In attempting to write the diphthong /aɪ/ as in *baile* he may use the English spelling, *ile* and thus write **bile*.

Reading problem: In reading such Spanish words as *vine, dime, dile, dice,* which are pronounced with /i/ in Spanish, the English speaker may interpret them as containing the diphthong /aɪ/.

2.3 *Comparing two systems that use different alphabets but with some symbols that are similar.* English and Russian constitute a good example. English uses the Latin alphabet; Russian uses the Cyrillic alphabet. Some letters in these two alphabets are similar enough in form to be identified as same by speakers of one language learning to write and read the other.

The following transliteration scheme from Russian letters to phonemic symbols shows the main symbols of the Russian writing system and the sounds they represent. The Russian letter is the first member of each pair.

CYRILLIC ALPHABET WITH FREQUENT PHONEMIC EQUIVALENT

а	a	и	i	р	r	ш	š
б	b	й	y(1)	с	s	щ	šč
в	v	к	k	т	t	ъ	(2)
г	g	л	l	у	u	ы	ï
д	d	м	m	ф	f	ь	j(3)
е	yɛ	н	n	х	x	э	ɛ
ж	ž	о	o	ц	c	ю	yu
з	z	п	p	ч	č	я	ya

(1) used in forming diphthongs.
(2) used to denote certain morpheme boundaries.
(3) indicates palatalization of preceding consonant.

A glance at these symbols immediately reveals many problems for the English speaker learning to write and read Russian.

(a) *Foreign language symbols not found in the native language.*
There are a good number of these. Notice some obvious examples:
ж, з, л, ф, э, ю. The English writer will have to learn to draw
these, and, with practice, to write them and read them with in-
creasing ease. Rarely will he use them with the ease of a native
who has been writing them since childhood.

(b) *Symbols that are similar enough to the native ones to be
identified with them.* There are a good number of these also.
Obvious examples are в, г, е, и, к, м, н, о, р, с, т, у, н, ь.
Less obvious examples might be б, д, ц, ч, ъ, я, The English
speaker will have minor difficulty with these symbols when they
are not identical to the English ones.

(c) *Similar symbols that represent different sounds.* Of the
symbols that are similar in the two languages some represent
sounds that are more or less similar also. The student will have
practically no difficulty learning those. Other similar symbols,
however, represent quite different sounds in the two languages.
The most striking examples are

г	representing [g]	ь	representing [j]
и	representing [i]	д	representing [d]
н	representing [n]	ц	representing [c]
р	representing [r]	ч	representing [č]
у	representing [u]	ъ	representing [w]
ы	representing [ï]	я	representing [ä]

These symbols constitute a learning burden.

Writing problem: The English writer will tend to use the
English letters commonly used to represent the sounds which are
similar to [g, i, n, r, u, y, j, d, c, č, w, ä] Thus he might want
to write *noon* for Russian *HyH* [nun].

Reading problem: He will tend to read the Russian letters
with the sounds the similar English letters would have. Example:
Russian *HyH* might be read as *[haɪ].

The Russian speaker learning to read English would have
similar problems though not the same ones. There is no added
illustrative value in showing the comparison with English as the
foreign language, and we shall not present it here.

2.4 *Comparing two alphabetic writing systems that show no
obvious resemblances.* Even though Korean writing may at first
glance seem to resemble Chinese writing, it is actually an alphabetic system and not a logographic writing system such as that of
Chinese. Korean written symbols represent sounds much as

English writing does. In fact, Korean writing is more consistent in its representation of sounds than is English.

KOREAN ALPHABET WITH BROAD PHONETIC EQUIVALENTS

ㅏ	a	ㅡ	ï	ㅘ	wa	ㅅ	s
ㅑ	ya	ㅣ	i	ㅝ	wɔ	ㅇ	ŋ
ㅓ	ɔ	ㅐ	æ	ㄱ	[k,g]	ㅈ	j
ㅕ	yɔ	ㅒ	yæ	ㄴ	n	ㅊ	č
ㅗ	o	ㅔ	ε	ㄷ	[t,d]	ㅋ	kʰ
ㅛ	yo	ㅖ	yε	ㄹ	[l,r]	ㅌ	tʰ
ㅜ	u	ㅙ	wε	ㅁ	m	ㅍ	pʰ
ㅠ	yu	ㅟ	wi	ㅂ	[p,b]	ㅎ	h

BASIC CONSONANT-VOWEL WRITTEN COMBINATIONS

가 나 다 라 마 바 사 아 자 차 카 타 파 하
갸 냐 댜 랴 먀 뱌 샤 야 쟈 챠 캬 탸 퍄 햐
거 너 더 러 머 버 서 어 저 처 커 터 퍼 허
겨 녀 뎌 려 며 벼 셔 여 져 쳐 켜 텨 펴 혀
교 노 도 로 모 보 소 오 조 초 코 토 포 호
꾜 뇨 됴 료 묘 뵤 쇼 요 죠 쵸 쿄 툐 표 효
구 누 두 루 무 부 수 우 주 추 쿠 투 푸 후
규 뉴 듀 류 뮤 뷰 슈 유 쥬 츄 큐 튜 퓨 휴
그 느 드 르 므 브 스 으 즈 츠 크 트 프 흐
기 니 디 리 미 비 시 이 지 치 키 티 피 히

Korean writing is a good example of an alphabetic system with symbols that do not resemble those of the Latin alphabet used in English. Above are the symbols of the Korean alphabet paired with the sounds they represent. The sounds are given in a modified International Phonetic Alphabet. (A table of useful phonetic and phonemic symbols is given in the appendix.) Modern Korean like English is written from left to right.

The English speaker learning to write Korean has to learn to write the symbols of the Korean alphabet as a separate undertaking, a problem that does not exist between English and Spanish. Similarly, the Korean speaker learning to write English has the problem of learning to write the Latin alphabet. Between English and Korean there will be no major negative transfer such as would result if some symbols were similar but represented different sounds. And there will be no positive transfer as when similar symbols represent similar sounds.

The learning burden seems less, however, than that for a Korean or English speaking child learning to write his own language. Learning to write his first language he has to master the great abstraction involved in representing the sounds of a language by marks on paper. Learning to write a second language, he already knows that marks on paper can represent sounds, and, as a matter of fact, he expects the marks to represent the phonemes of the second language.

The Thai writing system bears no resemblance to the Latin alphabet or the Korean alphabet, but it is also an alphabetic system; that is, the symbols represent phonemes. Following are the Thai symbols paired with the sounds they usually represent. The sounds are given in modified I. P. A. The line of writing proceeds from left to right as in the Latin and Korean alphabets.

Because Thai is a tone language there are symbols for the tones. If, as we have assumed, the student learns to speak the language first, there should be no particular difficulty in learning to use the symbols for pitch phonemes. The problems of an English student learning to read and write Thai and of a Thai student learning to read and write English parallel those for Korean and English and will therefore not be illustrated further.

Arabic exemplifies a variation of the problem. Arabic symbols represent sounds but with two important differences. First, Arabic writing usually omits the short vowels and represents only the consonants and long vowels. In teaching children, however, and in the Koran and the Bible, all the vowel symbols are used. Second, Arabic is written and read from right to left. The first difference might potentially be a major one, but in practice

THAI ALPHABET WITH
APPROXIMATE PHONETIC SYMBOLS

Thai	Phon.	Thai	Phon.	Thai	Phon.
-ั	a	เ-าะ	ɔ	ซ, ส, ศ, ษ	s
-า	a:	-อ	ɔ:	ญ, ย	y
-ิ	ɪ	ัวะ	ua	ด, ฎ	d
-ี	ɪ:	ัว	ua:	ต, ฏ	t
-ึ	ɨ	เ-ียะ	ia	ฐ, ฑ, ฒ, ถ, ท, ธ	tʰ
-ื	ɨ:	เ-ีย	ia:	น ณ	n
-ุ	u	เ-ือะ	ɨa	บ	b
-ู	u:	เ-ือ	ɨa:	ป	p
เ-ะ	e	ำ	am	ฝ, ฟ	f
เ-	e:	ไ-, ใ-	ay	ภ, พ, ผ	pʰ
แ-ะ	æ	เ-า	aw	ม	m
แ-	æ:	ก	k	ร	r
เ-อะ	ə	ข, ค, ฆ	kʰ	ล, ฬ	l
เ-อ	ə:	ง	ŋ	ว	w
โ-ะ	o	จ	j	ฮ, ห	h
โ-	o:	ฉ, ช, ฌ	č		

it is not, because Arabic-speaking children have used vowel symbols in learning to read and write Arabic and they will most probably have read the symbols in the Koran or Bible. They will therefore not be confused by the practice of including vowels in English writing. The second difference, that of writing from right to left, is more important than might be suspected. Arabic students learning to write English show the effects of this difference in the appearance and speed of their handwriting. Even reasonably advanced students write English slowly, and their work looks insecure and hesitant. This difference in the direction of writing is also a factor in the slower reading of English by Arabic speakers and even Persian speakers, who although speaking a language related to English because it is Indo-European, use the Arabic alphabet.

Following are Arabic symbols and approximate phonetic sounds they usually represent.

ARABIC ALPHABET WITH PHONEMIC SYMBOLS

ا	ʔ , a:	خ	kh[x]	ش	š	غ	ġ	ن	n
ب	b	د	d	ص	ṣ	ف	f	ه	h
ت	t	ذ	ð	ض	ḍ	ق	q	و	w,u:
ث	θ	ر	r	ط	ṭ	ك	k	ى	y,i:
ج	ǰ	ز	z	ظ	ẓ	ل	l	´	a
									i
ح	ḥ	س	s	ع	ʕ	م	m	´	u

2.5 *Comparing two writing systems which are basically different.* Chinese writing as compared with any alphabetic system is the classic example. Chinese writing does not represent sounds. It represents Chinese words or morphemes. In learning to write Chinese, the alphabetically habituated person simply has to start afresh. He will be very slow at grasping words through the Chinese characters that represent them. And he will be even slower at writing them. He will forget the symbols that represent the words he wants to write, and he will forget the words represented by the symbols he wants to read. He will be further handicapped by having to read vertically down and in columns from right to left. If he learns to write Chinese as an adult he may never attain the same ease, speed, and flexibility that the Chinese speaker who learned to read and write early may have attained.

If, as in the case of Japanese, the system includes syllabic writing as well as Chinese characters, the problem of learning the syllabary will be more like that of learning new letters than the learning of logographs (which in Japanese happen to be Chinese logographs). On the one hand, the total number of symbols to be learned in writing Japanese is smaller than if everything were written in Chinese characters. On the other hand, the problem of learning a complex system, using syllabic writing for some things and Chinese characters for others, has to be reckoned an added burden.

A syllabary has more symbols than an alphabet, since obviously there are more syllables than phonemes in a language. If the English-speaking student were learning a completely syllabic system, such as that of Cherokee, however, the learning burden would be definitely much lighter than learning to write Chinese. The number of symbols to be learned is quite small (85) compared to the number of characters to be learned for Chinese. And learning to represent syllables is more like learning to represent phonemes than words. In Cherokee there will also be some positive and negative transfer resulting from similarity of symbols to those of English.

3. Application.

3.1 With the results of the kind of comparison illustrated above, we can sharpen our teaching of the writing system of a foreign language quite dramatically. Clarification and practice can easily be focused on the problems to be found by the student. And the challenge of these difficulties, when clearly understood, can be a surprisingly strong incentive for concentrated study.

The necessary compactness of testing instruments can best be achieved by using the results of our analysis of problems. And research problems can be made much more significant and much less bulky by the same means.

Finally, we may better understand that the hesitant handwriting of a foreign writer does not reflect weakness of character or childishness or immaturity, but a shift to a new system where the habits of his own writing do not operate, or may even operate as a negative force.

Chapter 6

HOW TO COMPARE TWO CULTURES

1. Introduction.

1.1 *On culture.* "Culture," as we understand it here, is synonymous with the "ways of a people." As such it is the least understood of all the matters discussed in this volume. More often than not the ways of a people are praised by that same people while looked upon with suspicion or disapproval by the others, and often in both cases with surprisingly little under-standing of what those ways really are and mean.

When a visitor is in the United States to study the American way of life or American culture, almost everyone is glad to show him that way and that culture, but what do we show him and what do we tell him? How do we know what to show and tell him?

If we are near an automobile plant, we will show him of course an assembly line and the tourist spots in the city. And perhaps we will show him a farm and a school. And we will tell him the favorable generalities that we have been taught about ourselves, which may happen to be the same favorable generalities he too has learned about himself and his culture. Occasionally someone among us wishing to pose as a detached intellectual may criticize a thing or two, or everything. But we are really rather helpless to interpret ourselves accurately and to describe what we do, because we have grown up doing it and we do much of what we do through habit, acquired almost unnoticed from our elders and our cultural environment.

Our inability to describe our cultural ways parallels our in-ability to describe our language, unless we have made a special study of it. The paradox is that we are able to use the complex structure that is our language with astonishing ease and flexi-bility, but when someone asks us when to use *between* and *among,* for example, we will tell him the most surprising fiction with the best intention of telling the truth. Similarly, we may be able to tie a bow tie with speed and ease, but the moment someone asks us to explain what we do, we become thoroughly confused and may give him completely false information. We describe ourselves as being free and at the same time may demand that our student visitors attend class regularly, a restriction that is considered an invasion of personal freedom in some countries.

110

We cannot hope to compare two cultures unless we have more accurate understanding of each of the cultures being compared. We must be able to eliminate the things we claim to do but actually don't do. We must be able to describe the things we do without being conscious of doing them, and we must make sure we are able to describe practices accurately, not haphazardly or ideally. And we must be able to describe the situations in which we do what we do.

1.2 *Definition of culture.* I assume with others that cultures are structured systems of patterned behavior. Following is a good definition given by anthropologists.

> Cultural anthropologists, during the last twenty-five years, have grad-
> ually moved from an atomistic definition of culture, describing it as a
> more or less haphazard collection of traits, to one which emphasizes
> pattern and configuration. Kluckhohn and Kelly perhaps best express
> this modern concept of culture when they define it as 'all those histori-
> cally created designs for living explicit and implicit, rational, irrational,
> and non-rational, which exist at any given time as potential guides for
> the behavior of men.' Traits, elements, or, better, patterns of culture
> in this definition are organized or structured into a system or set of
> systems, which, because it is historically created, is therefore open
> and subject to constant change.[1]

Compare also the statement by Edward Sapir that "All cultural behavior is patterned."[2]

1.3 *Functioning units of a culture.* The individual acts of behavior through which a culture manifests itself are never ex- actly alike. Each act is unique, and the very same act never occurs again. Even in performing a play many times, each act performed by the player is unique, and it can be shown to be dif- ferent from the "same" act in the very next performance. Yet in every culture certain acts which in physical terms are thus dif- ferent are nevertheless accepted as same. Having orange juice, coffee, fried eggs, and white toast one morning and grapefruit juice, coffee, scrambled eggs, and whole wheat toast the next morning would usually be considered in the United States two occurrences of the same unit of behavior: eating breakfast. Yet they are different. The mold or design into which certain acts must fall to be considered breakfast in the United States consti- tutes a pattern of behavior, a functioning unit of behavior in that

---

[1]Harry Hoijer, "The Relation of Language to Culture," in *Anthropology Today*, ed. A. L. Kroeber (Chicago: Univ. Chi. Press, 1953) p. 554.
[2]"The Status of Linguistics as a Science," *Selected Writings of Edward Sapir*, ed. David G. Mandelbaum (Berkeley and Los Angeles: Univ. Calif. Press, 1949) p. 546.

culture. These patterns are in turn made up of substitutible elements such as performer, act, objects, setting, time, manner, purpose, etc. These elements, though always unique and always different, are identified into "sames" and "differents" within certain molds which are cultural patterns also. These sames have characteristic features in each culture and they are usually of various classes. One such class in many cultures consists of items treated as static units, for example, men, women, children, doctor, nurse, teacher, barber, animals, horses, dogs, ghosts, witches, goblins, ideas, family, club, church, school, factory, store, farm, tree, building, museum, house, etc. Another class is constituted by items treated as processes, for example, to rest, to study, to fish, to run, to think, to sit, to die, etc. Still another includes items treated as qualities, as for example, fast, slow, good, bad, hot, cold, sleepy, sleepily, cruel, constructively, fishy, etc.

1.4 *Form, meaning, and distribution.* Such units of patterned behavior, which constitute the designs that are each culture, have form, meaning, and distribution. [3]

---

[3] These three dimensions are not the same as Pike's three modes. Compare Pike, "...on any level of focus each such emic unit, each chunk, even one for which the borders seem relatively clear cut, is divided structurally into three specific kinds of complex overlapping components which I shall call MODES.... (p. 35)

"If we symbolize an emic unit of activity as U, the feature mode as F, the manifestation mode as M, and the distribution mode as D, then any emic unit of any type on any level of focus is defined completely as:

$$U = \begin{matrix} F \\ M \\ D \end{matrix}$$

This formula applies not only to emic units which are chunks of activity, but also to all special kinds of emic units such as emic classes. It is this fact which — the theory suggests — is at the heart of the nature of the structure of behavior (and perhaps of many other kinds of structure as well) and leads to its characteristic hierarchical appearance." (p. 40)

In my model, the *form* includes Pike's manifestation mode and feature mode; my *distribution* coincides somewhat with Pike's distribution mode. As to *meaning*, I need to consider it as a coequal element, whereas Pike does not mention meaning separately in his definition formula. He of course does not reject meaning. Cf., "In spite of the problems which are involved, it is absolutely essential, if one is to study behavior *as it actually functions*, that one assume that the analyst can detect the presence and to some degree the nature of meaning and purpose. It should be strongly emphasized, however, that this by no means implies that we assume that the analyst is able to detect meaning and purpose without error — rather it is assumed that he does so crudely, with a margin of indeterminacy and of error. Nevertheless his possible degree of accuracy is sufficiently high to enable him to utilize this feature of the morpheme and of the uttereme to help identify these units, provided that from the earliest stages of his analysis he always accompanies the study of this purposive-meaning component of the emic units with a study of the formal components of their physical activity, and attempts the analysis neither of form nor of meaning by itself without reference to the other." (p. 80) Kenneth L. Pike, *Language in Relation to a Unified Theory of the Structure of Human Behavior,* Part I, preliminary ed. (Glendale, Calif.: Summer Institute of Linguistics, 1954).

The forms of these patterns of culture are identified functionally on inspection by the members of that culture, although the same individuals may not be able accurately to define the very forms that they can identify. Even such a clear unit of behavior as eating breakfast, immediately identified by the performer if we ask him what he is doing, may be described by him as the morning meal or the meal when you eat cereal, bacon, eggs, and coffee, yet a man who works during the night might be eating his breakfast in the evening, and a meal of cereal, bacon, eggs, and coffee might be lunch or even supper.

What is breakfast then? Can we define it? Yes, but the point being made is that the very same individuals who can tell us without hesitation and with accuracy "I am eating breakfast" may not be able to define breakfast for us and may do it erroneously. We can describe breakfast by observing a representative number of occurrences of breakfast and by noting the contrasts with those occurrences which seem to resemble breakfast but are identified as lunch, dinner, a snack, or supper by natives.

Meanings, like forms, are culturally determined or modified. They represent an analysis of the universe as grasped in a culture. Patterned forms have a complex of meanings, some representing features of a unit or process or quality, some grasped as primary, others as secondary, tertiary, etc. Eating breakfast, lunch, and dinner are engaged in usually to provide food and drink for the body. We say then that breakfast, lunch, and dinner usually have that primary meaning. In addition a particular form of breakfast at a particular time or day may have a meaning of good or bad on a moral or religious scale, on a health scale, on an economic scale, etc. A particular form of breakfast may carry as secondary meaning a social-class identification, a national origin identification, a religious identification. In short, any of the distinctions and groupings of a culture may be part of the meaning of a particular form unit.

Distribution. All of these meaningful units of form are distributed in patterned ways. Their distribution patterns are complexes involving various time cycles, space locations, and positions in relation to other units. Breakfast, for example, shows time distribution on a daily cycle, a weekly cycle, and a yearly cycle. Breakfast shows a space or location distribution. It is also distributed after some units of behavior and preceding others.

Form, meaning, and distribution probably do not exist independent of each other in a culture, but they are spoken of operationally here as separate. Forms are relevant when they have meaning; meaning presupposes a form in order to be of relevance to us; and meaningful forms always occur in patterned distribution.

Within a culture we can assume that when an individual observes a significant patterned form in a patterned distribution spot, it will have a complex of culturally patterned meanings for him. Breakfast in the kitchen at 7 a. m., served by the same person who eats it, and including coffee, fruit juice, and cereal, will have a different complex of meanings than breakfast in bed at 11 a. m. served by a formally dressed waiter, and including caviar and other trimmings.

It may be worth pointing out at this time that the observation of a form may occur directly, indirectly through still photography, motion pictures, television, etc., or indirectly again by means of a language report.

1.5 *Transfer to a foreign culture.* The patternings that make it possible for unique occurrences to operate as sames among the members of a culture did not develop for operation across cultures. When they do occur in contact across cultures, many instances of predictable misinterpretation take place. We can assume that when the individual of culture A trying to learn culture B observes a form in culture B in a particular distribution spot, he grasps the same complex of meaning as in his own culture. And when he in turn engages actively in a unit of behavior in culture B he chooses the form which he would choose in his own culture to achieve that complex of meaning.

2. Comparison of Cultures.

2.1 If the native culture habits are transferred when learning a foreign culture, it is obvious that, by comparing the two culture systems, we can predict what the trouble spots will be. Obviously, this is a huge undertaking, and we will present a few examples that may facilitate cultural analysis and comparison.

2.2 *Same form, different meaning.* We will expect trouble when the same form has different classification or meaning in the two cultures.

2.2.1 A very interesting kind of trouble spot is seen when any element of the form of a complex pattern has different classification or meaning across cultures. The foreign observer gives to the entire pattern the meaning of that different classification of one element.

Example. Bullfighting has always been in my observation a source of cross-cultural misinformation. It is a particularly

difficult pattern of behavior to explain convincingly to an unso-
phisticated United States observer. I therefore choose it as a
test case.

Form. A bullfight has a very precise, complex form. A man,
armed with a sword and a red cape, challenges and kills a fighting bull. The form is prescribed in great detail. There are
specific vocabulary terms for seemingly minute variations. The
bullfighter, the bull, the picadors, the music, the dress, etc. are
part of the form.

Meaning. The bullfight has a complex of meaning in Spanish
culture. It is a sport. It symbolizes the triumph of art over the
brute force of a bull. It is entertainment. It is a display of
bravery.

Distribution. The bullfight shows a complex distribution pattern. There is a season for bullfights on a yearly cycle, there
are favored days on a weekly cycle, and there is a favored time
on a daily cycle. The bullfight occurs at a specific place, the
bull ring, known to the least person in the culture.

Form, meaning, and distribution to an alien observer. An
American observer seated next to a Spanish or Mexican spectator
will see a good deal of the form, though not all of it. He will see
a man in a special dress, armed with a sword and cape, challenging and killing the bull. He will see the bull charging at the man
and will notice that the man deceives the bull with his cape. He
will notice the music, the color, etc.

The meaning of the spectacle is quite different to him, however. It is the slaughter of a "defenseless" animal by an armed
man. It is unfair because the bull always gets killed. It is
unsportsmanlike — to the bull. It is cruel to animals. The fighter
is therefore cruel. The public is cruel.

The distribution constitutes no particular problem to the
American observer, since he has the experience of football,
baseball, and other spectacles.

Misinformation. Is there an element of misinformation here,
and if so, wherein is it? I believe there is misinformation. The
secondary meaning "cruel" is found in Spanish culture, but it does
not attach to the bullfight. The American observer ascribing the
meaning cruel to the spectator and fighter is getting information
that is not there. Why?

Since the cruelty is interpreted by the American observer as
being perpetrated by the man on the bull, we can test to see if
those parts of the complex form — the bull and the man — are the
same in the two cultures.

Linguistic evidence. We find evidence in the language that

seems interesting.[4] A number of vocabulary items that are applicable both to animals and to humans in English have separate words for animals and for humans in Spanish. In English both animals and persons have *legs*. In Spanish, animals have *patas* 'animal legs' and humans have *piernas* 'human legs.' Similarly, in English, animals and humans have *backs* and *necks*, while in Spanish, animals have *lomo* and *pescuezo* 'animal back' and 'animal neck' and humans have *espalda* and *cuello* 'human back' and 'human neck.' Furthermore, in English, both animals and humans *get nervous*, have *hospitals*, and have *cemeteries*, named by means of various metaphors. In Spanish, animals do not get nervous, or have hospitals or cemeteries. The linguistic evidence, though only suggestive, points to a difference in the classification of *animal* in the two cultures.[5] In Hispanic culture the distinction between man and animal seems very great, certainly greater than that in American culture.

By further observation of what people say and do one finds additional features of difference. In Spanish culture, man is not

---

[4]Cf. Edward Sapir, "Language is becoming increasingly valuable as a guide to the scientific study of a given culture. In a sense, the network of cultural patterns of a civilization is indexed in the language which expresses that civilization. It is an illusion to think that we can understand the significant outlines of a culture through sheer observation and without the guide of the linguistic symbolism which makes these outlines significant and intelligible to society....

"Language is a guide to 'social reality.' Though language is not ordinarily thought of as of essential interest to the students of social science, it powerfully conditions all our thinking about social problems and processes. Human beings do not live in the objective world alone, nor alone in the world of social activity as ordinarily understood, but are very much at the mercy of the particular language which has become the medium of expression for their society.... The fact of the matter is that the 'real world' is to a large extent unconsciously built up on the language habits of the group.... We see and hear and otherwise experience very largely as we do because the language habits of our community predispose certain choices of interpretation." *Op. cit.*, pp. 161-62.

Cf. also Harry Hoijer, "It is evident from these statements [quoted from Sapir and Whorf], if they are valid, that language plays a large and significant role in the totality of culture. Far from being simply a technique of communication, it is itself a way of directing the perceptions of its speakers and it provides for them habitual modes of analyzing experience into significant categories. And to the extent that languages differ markedly from each other, so should we expect to find significant and formidable barriers to cross-cultural communication and understanding." "The Sapir-Whorf Hypothesis," in *Language in Culture*, ed. Harry Hoijer (Chicago: Univ. Chi. Press, 1954) p. 94.

[5]Cf. Joseph H. Greenberg, "The existence of distinct E.M.U's [Elementary Meaning Units] makes us suspect a difference in response to the situations designated by the terms. It does not, in general, tell us the nature of this difference in response. For example, the existence of separate unanalyzable terms for father's brother and mother's brother makes us posit a difference in reaction to these relatives. It does not tell us wherein the difference consists, whether, for example, the first is treated with deference but the second with familiarity. To discover this, we must observe behavior, both verbal and nonverbal, that is, what things are habitually said and done with reference to the father's brother and the mother's brother." "Concerning Inferences from Linguistic to Nonlinguistic Data," in *Language in Culture*, ed., Harry Hoijer (Chicago: Univ. Chi. Press, 1954) pp. 9-10.

physically strong but is skillful and intelligent. A bull is strong
but not skillful and not intelligent. In American culture a man is
physically strong, and so is a bull. A bull is intelligent. A bull
has feelings of pain, sorrow, pity, tenderness — at least in animal
stories such as that of *Ferdinand the Bull*.[6] A bull deserves an
even chance in a fight; he has that sportsman's right even against
a man.

We can, then, hypothesize that the part of the complex form
represented by the bull has a different classification, a different
meaning, in American culture, and that herein lies the source of
the misinformation.

We should test this hypothesis by minimal contrast if possible.
We find something akin to a minimal contrast in American culture
in tarpon fishing. In tarpon fishing we have a form: a fight to
the exhaustion and death of the tarpon at the hands of a man with
a line and camouflaged hooks. Much of the form is prescribed in
detail. There is no large visible audience, but newspaper stories
in a sense represent audience contact. In the complex of meaning, it is a sport, and it represents a triumph of skill over the
brute fighting strength of the fish. The distribution seems somewhat different from that of a bullfight, but the difference does not
seem relevant as an explanation of the difference we have hy-
pothesized.

We now observe that the very same American who interpreted
the bullfight as cruel, and applied that meaning to the spectator
and the bullfighter, will sit next to the same spectator on a fishing boat and never think of the fishing game as cruel. I conclude
that the part of the complex form represented by the fish is quite
distinct from "human being" in both American and Spanish cultures, while the part identified as the bull is much more like
"human being" in American culture than in Spanish culture.

Marginal supporting evidence is the fact that in American culture there is a Society for the Prevention of Cruelty to Animals
which concerns itself with the feelings of dogs, cats, horses, and
other domestic animals. Recently there was a front-page story
in the local papers reporting that the Humane Society of New
York City had sent a Santa Claus to distribute gifts among the
dogs in the New York City pounds. We would not conceive of a
society for the prevention of cruelty to fish.

2.2.2 A form in culture B, identified by an observer from
culture A as the same form as one in his own culture, actually
has a different meaning.

---

[6]Well known motion picture prepared by Walt Disney Studies, from a children's story.

Example. A hiss, a sharp, voiceless sibilant sound, expresses disapproval in the United States. In Spanish-speaking countries it is the normal way to ask for silence in a group. Fries reports being taken aback the first time he faced a Spanish-speaking audience and heard them "hissing." He wondered if they were hissing at him. Later he learned that they were calling for silence.[7]

Example. Drinking milk at meals is a standard practice in the United States. To us it has a primary meaning of food and drink, standard drink, at meal time. It does not have any special connotation of social class, national group, religious group, age group, or economic stratum. Wine, on the other hand, may be served on special occasions or by special groups of the population who have had special contacts with other cultures. Wine, thus, has the meanings special occasion, special group of people.

In France, milk at meals is not the standard drink. Some children may drink milk, some adults may drink milk for special reasons, some individuals or families or groups may drink milk because of special cultural contacts. Drinking milk at meals in France has the secondary meanings of special drink, special occasion, or special group of people. Its primary meaning would be food and drink for the body.

The reader may recall the sensation that former Premier Pierre Mendes-France caused in the United States when he began measures to extend the drinking of milk in France. Everybody recalls the favorable impression he made in the United States by drinking milk in public. Now, discounting those who may be familiar with scientific studies on the relative food value of milk as against wine, I take it that there was cross-cultural misinformation, and that there will be trouble in understanding another culture in similar cases. To the American public, Mendes-France was rescuing the French people from the special habit of drinking wine and teaching them the standard, wholesome practice of drinking milk.

2.3 *Same meaning, different form.* We can expect another kind of trouble spot when the same meaning in two cultures is associated with different forms. The alien observer seeking to act in the culture being learned will select his own form to achieve the meaning, and he may miss altogether the fact that a different form is required.

Example. A young man from Izfahan, Iran, gets off the

---

[7]Charles C. Fries, "American Linguistics and the Teaching of English," *Language Learning,* 6, Nos. 1 and 2 (1955), 17.

train in a small town of the United States. He claims his baggage and attempts to hail a taxi. A likely car with a white license plate and black letters goes by. The young man waves at it. The car does not stop. Another car appears with the same type of license plate. The young man waves again, without success. Frustrated because in the United States taxis will not stop for him, he picks up his suitcases and walks to his destination. He later finds out that taxis in the United States are distinguished not by a white license plate, but by bright flashing lights and loud colors. In Izfahan at that time the signal for a taxi was a white license plate. This was an intelligent university-level student stumbling over a predictable type of problem.

We can expect further trouble in the fact that the members of one culture usually assume that their way of doing things, of understanding the world around them, their forms and their meanings, are the correct ones. Hence, when another culture uses other forms or other meanings it is wrong. Hence, when another culture adopts a pattern of behavior from the first one, the imitated culture feels that something good and correct is taking place.

Example. When foreign visitors from areas where coffee is served very black and very strong taste American coffee, they do not say that it is different; they say that American coffee is bad. Likewise, when Americans go abroad to countries where coffee is black and strong, they taste the coffee and do not say that it is different; they, too, say that it is bad.

Example. When Americans go abroad during the cold season, they complain that houses are cold. We often think that such cold houses cannot be good for one's health. When foreign visitors spend a winter in the colder areas of the United States, on the other hand, they complain that our houses are kept too hot and that the changes in temperature when going in and out of houses must be bad for one's health.

2.4 *Same form, same meaning, different distribution.* There is trouble in learning a foreign culture when a pattern that has the same form and the same meaning shows different distribution. The observer of a foreign culture assumes that the distribution of a pattern in the observed culture is the same as in his native culture, and therefore on noticing more of, less of, or absence of a feature in a single variant he generalizes his observation as if it applied to all variants and therefore to the entire culture. Distribution is a souce of a great many problems.

Example. For some time it was puzzling to me that on the one hand Latin American students complained that North American

meals abused the use of sugar, while on the other hand the dieti-
tians complained that Latin Americans used too much sugar at
meals. How could these seemingly contradictory opinions be
true at the same time? We can observe that the average Latin
American student takes more sugar in his coffee than do North
Americans. He is not used to drinking milk at meals, but when
milk is served he sometimes likes to put sugar in it. The dietitian notices this use of sugar in situations in which North Americans would use less or none at all. The dietitian notices also
that the sugar bowls at tables where Latin Americans sit have to
be filled more often than at other tables. She therefore feels
quite confident in making her generalization.

The Latin American student for his part finds a salad made of
sweet gelatin, or half a canned pear on a lettuce leaf. Sweet
salad! He may see beans for lunch — a treat! He sits at the
table, all smiles (I have watched the process), he takes a good
spoonful and, sweet beans! They are Boston baked beans. Turkey is served on Thanksgiving Day, but when the Latin American
tastes the sauce, he finds that it is sweet — it is cranberry sauce.
Sweet sauce for broiled turkey! That is the limit — these North
Americans obviously use too much sugar in their food. And
whatever secondary meanings are attached to too much sugar in
a person's diet tend to be attached to the people of the country
who prepare and eat such meals.

Another type of problem related to distribution differences,
or rather to assumed distribution differences, occurs when members of one culture, who normally recognize many subgroups in
the population of their own culture, assume that another culture
with which they come in contact is uniform. Hence, observations
made about one individual of that other culture tend to be generalized to the entire population.

Example. Folk opinions abroad about the morals of American
women are partly connected with this assumed uniformity of population and partly, too, with the fact that the same form may have
different meanings in the two cultures. Those who see American
movies or come in contact with American tourists often misinterpret the forms of the behavior they observe, and often also
they ascribe to the whole culture, the whole population, what may
well be restricted to a special group on a special distribution
spot. We in turn often ascribe to French and other Latin cultures
moral behavior that may be restricted to special samples coming
in contact with special visitors.

2.5 *Preconceived notions.* The notions filtered through the
above types of misinformation and through others becomes part

of the native culture as its "correct" view of the reality of the foreign one, and as young members grow up they receive these views as truth through verbal reports and all the other vehicles of enculturation. These preconceived notions constitute very serious obstacles to the understanding of another culture.

3. Gathering Cultural Data for a Structural Description.

3.1 Since good structural descriptions of the cultures that may require our attention will usually not be found ready-made, we present below a checklist of possible patterns of behavior that in various cultures constitute functioning units. This checklist may be helpful in calling attention to areas that might otherwise go unnoticed.

To prepare for a comparison of another culture with the native one it may be valuable to use the informant approach coupled with systematic observation of the culture in its normal undisturbed operation.

One can interview representative informants who are articulate enough to talk about what they do. We can ask them what they do each day of a typical week and on the various special days of the month and year. We can ask them what is done on the special days of the various turning points in the life cycle, that is, birth, growing up, courtship and marriage, raising their young, retiring, dying.

What the informant reports may be classified for easier grasp and later verification and comparison into things he does to meet the needs of his body: sleep and rest, food and drink, shelter, clothing, exercise, healing, cleanliness, etc.; things he does to meet the needs of his personality: artistic activities, social activities, study for the sake of knowing, etc.; and things he does to meet the needs of his soul: religious activities. Other things may more conveniently be classified as tool activities: transportation, communication, work, training, organizations, government, etc. These groupings do not imply valid cultural categories or units. Quite often a pattern of behavior, a structural unit such as marriage, will involve the body, the personality, the soul, and tool activities.

One must not make the mistake of generalizing on inadequate sampling. The informants should represent at least the major significant groups of the population. In describing a culture as complex as that of the United States one should see that what a religious person does on Sunday is not generalized to all religious groups and much less to the nonreligious members of the culture.

3.2 *Looking for structure.* Merely describing what any number of informants do in a culture does not constitute a structural description of the culture. Some of the things done will not be significant; that is, whether they are done or not or whether they are done one way or another will not change the unit of behavior. Other things, those we are interested in, will be significant: that is, doing something else will mean something else.

One must test variations to see if a change in meaning correlates with them. For example, we would observe that people sleep in a given culture and that they sleep in all cultures. We might observe that, say, in culture A most of our informants slept from between nine and eleven at night to between six and eight in the morning. We would check to see what would be thought of a person who habitually slept from one in the morning to eleven. We might find that the person would be considered lazy, or rich and lazy, or sick. The time of sleep would therefore be considered structurally significant. If the reaction were that sleeping those hours was all right because the person liked those hours, we would consider the time of sleeping not structurally significant.

Still checking on the pattern of sleep, one might observe in culture B that most of the informants slept or rested after the midday meal. One can check to see if not sleeping or resting at that time would have any particular meaning. If we found that people who did not rest at that time would be considered reckless with their health, overly ambitious, or foreigners or foreign-influenced, we would consider the afternoon nap a significant type of rest pattern.

Similarly, if the informants in culture A do not sleep or rest after the noon meal, we might check for the meaning to them of a member of their culture that sleeps afternoons. If he is considered lazy, or sick, or a weakling, we would take it that not sleeping after lunch was part of the rest structure in that culture.

In that same culture A if we found that one of the informants slept regularly during the day and worked during the night, would it have any special meaning? It probably would. The meaning might be that the informant was a night watchman or had to work on a night shift at the factory.

We can illustrate this search for structure with eating patterns or any other patterns in the culture we seek to understand. If an informant in culture A eats fish on Friday, would he also eat meat? If he would not eat meat, it might be for a religious reason.

3.3 Systematic observation of the culture in operation will do much to eliminate the errors that the interviews will inevitably introduce in our data. Testing in various ways for significance will also help us eliminate useless information as well as errors.

Even though a total analysis and comparison of any two highly complex cultures may not be readily available for some time to come, the kind of model and sample comparison discussed in this chapter will be helpful in interpreting observations made in the actual contact of persons of one culture with another culture.

APPENDIX

TABLE OF PHONETIC AND PHONEMIC SYMBOLS USED IN TEXT

SYM-BOL	EXAMPLES OR DESCRIPTION	SYM-BOL	EXAMPLES OR DESCRIPTION
i	beet	r	read, three
ɪ	bit	l	lead, deal
e	late, chaotic	h	hit
ɛ	let	w	wit
æ	fat, hat, man	y	yes
a	father, colony	kh[x]	voiceless velar fricative
ə	cut, above	ḥ	voiceless pharingeal fricative
ɨ	a high central vowel	ṣ	velarized [s]
ɔ	caught, all	ẓ	velarized [z]
o	note	ḍ	velarized [d]
u	pull	ṭ	velarized [t]
u	pool	q	voiceless uvular stop
p	pet, capture	c	[ts]
b	bet	g̃	voiced velar fricative
m	met	j	palatalizes preceding consonant
t	teach, bet, better	ɨ	high back unrounded vowel
d	do, good	ʔ	glottal stop
n	not	ʕ	voiced pharingeal fricative
k	coat	:	length mark
g	goat	/ /	Slant bars indicate phonemic
ŋ	ring		notation.
θ	think, ether	[ ]	Brackets indicate phonetic
ð	then, either		transcription without reference
f	fine		to phonemic structure.
v	vine		
s	sip, pass		
z	zipper, zoo		
š	ship, fashion		
ž	vision		
č	church		
ǰ	judge		

NOTE: Graphic symbols such as these give only a general clue to the sounds they represent. Each symbol actually stands for a considerable range of sounds in any one language and for even greater differences in different languages.

GENERAL BIBLIOGRAPHICAL INFORMATION[1]

For an introduction to modern linguistics, especially as it might have a bearing on foreign language learning, the following three titles may be read in the order given.

Sapir, Edward. *Language.*
Fries, Charles C. *Teaching and Learning English as a Foreign Language.*
Bloomfield, Leonard. *Language.*

Three articles by these same men are good introductory reading also:

Sapir, Edward, "Sound Patterns in Language."
Bloomfield, Leonard. *Outline Guide for the Practical Study of Foreign Languages.* (A monograph)
Fries, Charles C., "American Linguistics and the Teaching of English."

Other selected titles are given in the bibliography.

For technical training in the analysis of languages see:
Gleason, H. A., Jr. *An Introduction to Descriptive Linguistics.*
Bloch, Bernard, and Trager, George L. *Outline of Linguistic Analysis.*
Pike, Kenneth L. *Phonemics.*
--------. *Tone Languages.*
Nida, Eugene. *Morphemics.*

Journals carrying up-to-date articles and reviews on linguistics or applied linguistics are:

Language. Journal of the Linguistic Society of America.
Language Learning. A Journal of Applied Linguistics.
Word. Journal of the Linguistic Circle of New York.
Studies in Linguistics.
International Journal of American Linguistics.

Bibliographical resources will be found in the indexes of the journals listed above, appended to books and articles on linguistics and applied linguistics, in bibliographies on Romance linguistics and of other groups of languages, and in the following series:

---

[1] Complete information about the works listed in this section will be found in the Selected Bibliography.

Linguistic Bibliography for the Years 1939-1947. Permanent International Committee of Linguists. Two vols.

Linguistic Bibliography for the Year 1948 and Supplement for the Years 1939-1947. Permanent International Committee of Linguists.

Linguistic Bibliography for the Year 1949. Permanent International Committee of Linguists.

Linguistic Bibliography for the Year 1950. Permanent International Committee of Linguists.

Linguistic Bibliography for the Year 1951. Permanent International Committee of Linguists.

Linguistic Bibliography for the Year 1952. Permanent International Committee of Linguists.

Linguistic Bibliography for the Year 1953 with Supplement for Previous Years. Permanent International Committee of Linguists. Utrecht-Anvers: Spectrum, 1955.
This series is to be continued under similar titles.

Information about culture as patterned behavior, particularly with reference to language, will be found in:
Sapir, Edward. (ed. David G. Mandelbaum) *Selected Writings in Language, Culture and Personality.*
Kroeber, A. L., ed. *Anthropology Today.*
Hoijer, Harry, ed. *Language in Culture.*

SELECTED BIBLIOGRAPHY

I

Besterman, Theodore. *A World Bibliography of Bibliographies and of Bibliographical Catalogues, Calendars, Abstracts, Digests, Indexes, and the Like* (Third and final edition, revised and greatly enlarged throughout). Genève: Societas Bibliographica, 1955, Vols. I, II, A-N, xviii, 2858 pp. ·(Vol. III in preparation. See older editions.)

Bloch, Bernard, and Trager, George L. *Outline of Linguistic Analysis.* Baltimore: Linguistic Society of America, 1942 (reprinted 1950), 82 pp.

Bloomfield, Leonard. *Language.* New York: Henry Holt and Company, 1933, 564 pp.

--------. *Outline Guide for the Practical Study of Foreign Languages.* Baltimore: Linguistic Society of America, 1942, 16 pp.

--------. "Secondary and Tertiary Responses to Language," *Language*, 20, 45-55.

Carroll, John B. *The Study of Language; A Survey of Linguistics and Related Disciplines in America.* Cambridge, Mass.: Harvard University Press, 1953, 289 pp.

Fries, Charles C. *Teaching and Learning English as a Foreign Language.* Ann Arbor: University of Michigan Press, 1945, 153 pp.

--------. *The Structure of English; An Introduction to the Construction of English Sentences.* New York: Harcourt, Brace and Company, 1952, 304 pp.

--------. "American Linguistics and the Teaching of English," *Language Learning*, 6, Nos. 1 and 2 (1955), 1-22.

Gelb, Ignace J. *A Study of Writing: The Foundations of Grammatology.* Chicago: University of Chicago Press, 1952, 295 pp.

Gleason, H. A., Jr. *An Introduction to Descriptive Linguistics.* New York: Henry Holt and Company, 1955, 389 pp.

Hall, Robert A., Jr. "American Linguistics, 1925-1950," *Archivum Linguisticum*, 3, 101-25, and 4, 1-166. Also, "La linguistica americana del 1925 al 1950," *Ricerche Linguistiche*, 1 (1950), 273-302.

--------. *Leave Your Language Alone!* Ithaca, New York: Linguistica, 1950, 254 pp.

Haugen, Einar. "Problems of Bilingual Description," *Georgetown University Monograph Series on Languages and Linguistics.* No. 7 (1954), 9-19.

Hoijer, Harry (ed.). *Language in Culture* (Conference on the Interrelations of Language and Other Aspects of Culture). Chicago: University of Chicago Press, 1954, 286 pp.

International Phonetic Association. *The Principles of the International Phonetic Association, Being a Description of the International Phonetic Alphabet and the Manner of Using It.* London, 1949, 53 pp.

Joos, Martin. *Acoustic Phonetics* (Language Monographs, No. 23). Baltimore: Linguistic Society of America, 1948, 136 pp.

Kroeber, Alfred Louis (ed.). *Anthropology Today.* Chicago: University of Chicago Press, 1953, 966 pp.

Kurath, Hans. *Handbook of the Linguistic Geography of New England*. Providence: Brown University Press, 1939, 238 pp.

Martinet, Andre, and Weinreich, Uriel (eds.). *Linguistics Today* (Published on the occasion of the Columbia University Bicentennial). New York: Linguistic Circle of New York, Columbia University, 1954, v, 280 pp. (For the initiated.)

Meillet, Antoine, and Cohen, Marcel. *Les langues du monde* (rev. ed.). Paris: Champion, 1952, 1296 pp. plus maps.

Miller, George A. *Language and Communication*. New York: McGraw-Hill, 1951, 298 pp.

Nida, Eugene. *Morphology, The Descriptive Analysis of Words* (2d ed.). Ann Arbor: University of Michigan Press, 1949, 342 pp.

Pike, Kenneth L. *Phonemics; A Technique for Reducing Languages to Writing*. Ann Arbor: University of Michigan Press, 1947, 254 pp.

--------. *Tone Languages*. Ann Arbor: University of Michigan Press, 1948, 187 pp.

--------. *Language in Relation to a Unified Theory of the Structure of Human Behavior* (preliminary ed.). Glendale, California: Summer Institute of Linguistics. Part I, 1954, 170 pp; Part II, 1955, 85 pp.

Polivanov, E. "La perception des sons d'une language étrangère," *Travaux du Cercle Linguistique de Prague, 4.* Prague, 1931, pp. 79-96.

Pulgram, Ernst. "Phoneme and Grapheme: A Parallel," *Word*, 7, No. 1 (1951), 15-20.

Sapir, Edward. *Language; An Introduction to the Study of Speech*. New York: Harcourt, Brace and Company, 1921, 258 pp.

--------. "Sound Patterns in Language," *Language*, 1, No. 2, 37-51. Reprinted in *Language Learning*, 6, Nos. 3 and 4 (1956), 62-76.

II

SPECIFIC LANGUAGES AND COMPARISONS OF LANGUAGES (PARTIAL, SELECTED LIST)[2]

AMERICAN INDIAN LANGUAGES

Boas, Franz (ed.). *Handbook of American Indian Languages.* Washington, D.C., 1911.

Hoijer, Harry, and others. *Linguistic Structures of Native America.* New York: The Viking Fund Inc., 1946, 423 pp.

International Journal of American Linguistics.

ARABIC

Cantineau, Jean. "The Phonemic System of Damascus Arabic," *Word,* 12, No. 1 (1956): 116-124.

Ferguson, Charles A. "Book Reviews Syrian Arabic Studies," *Middle East Journal,* 9, No. 2 (1955), 187-94.

BULGARIAN

Andrejčin, Ljubomir, Kostov, Nikola, and Nikolov, En'o. *Bъlgarska gramatika,* pomogalo za ezikovo-gramatično obučenie v gimhaziite. Sofija: Dъržavno izdatelstvo pri Ministerstvo na Narodnoto Postveštenie, 1947, 331 pp.

BURMESE

Cornyn, William S. *Outline of Burmese Grammar.* Baltimore: Linguistic Society of America, 1944, 34 pp.

CHINESE

Chao, Yuen Ren. *Mandarin Primer.* Cambridge: Harvard

---

[2]Comparisons of languages appear only under the language to be learned. For example, a comparison of English and Arabic where English is the foreign language would appear only under English.

University Press, 1948. Vol. 1, viii, 336 pp; Vol. 2 (Character text for Mandarin Primer), viii, 142 pp.

Chao, Yuen Ren, and Yang, Lien Sheng. *Concise Dictionary of Spoken Chinese.* Cambridge, Mass.: Harvard University Press, 1947.

Fries, Charles C., and Shen, Yao. *Mandarin Chinese for English Speakers, An Oral Approach.* Ann Arbor: English Language Institute, University of Michigan, 1940. Vols. I-IV.

Hartman, Lawton M., III. "The Segmental Phonemes of the Peiping Dialect," *Language,* 20 (1944), 28-42.

Hockett, Charles F. "Peiping Phonology," *Journal of the American Oriental Society,* 67 (1947), 253-67.

--------. "Peiping Morphophonemics," *Language,* 26 (1950), 63-85.

Wong, Helen. "Outline of the Mandarin Phonemic System," *Word,* 9 (1953), 268-76.

--------. "Addenda et Corrigenda to 'Outline of the Mandarin Phonemic System,'" *Ibid.,* 10, No. 1 (1954), 71-72.

DANISH

Togeby, K. "Linguistics in Denmark: 1940-1948," *Symposium,* 3 (1949), 226-37. (Including phonetics and extensive bibliography.)

ENGLISH

American Speech: A Quarterly of Linguistic Usage. New York: Columbia University Press.

Bloomfield, Leonard. "Stressed Vowels of American English," *Language,* 11, 97-116.

Chatman, Seymour. "Some Problems in Teaching English Pronunciation to Persian Speakers," *Language Learning,* 4, Nos. 1 and 2 (1951-52), 36-41.

Cole, Luella. *The Teacher's Handbook of Technical Vocabulary.* Bloomington, Ill.: Public School Publishing Company, 1940, 144 pp.

Craigie, William A. *English Spelling, Its Rules and Reasons.* New York: F. S. Crofts & Co., 1927, viii, 115 pp.

Dale, Edgar (director). *Bibliography of Vocabulary Studies.* Columbus, Ohio: Bureau of Educational Research. The Ohio State University, 1949. v, 101 pp.

Dreher, John J. "A Comparison of Native and Acquired Intonation" Doctoral dissertation, University of Michigan. In *Microfilm Abstracts,* 11 (1951), 461. (Transfer from Chinese intonation to English.)

Eaton, Helen S. *Semantic Frequency List for English, French, German and Spanish: A Correlation of the First Six Thousand Words in Four Single-Language Frequency Lists* (issued by the Committee on Modern Languages of the American Council on Education). Chicago: Univ. Chi. Press, 1940, xxi, 441 pp.

Fries, Charles C. *American English Grammar: The Grammatical Structure of Present-day American English with Especial Reference to Social Differences or Class Dialects* (The Report of an Investigation Financed by the National Council of Teachers of English and Supported by the Modern Language Association and the Linguistic Society of America. National Council of Teachers of English, English Monograph No. 10.) New York: D. Appleton-Century Company, Inc., 1940, 313 pp. (Based on analysis of letters from whole range of social levels.)

--------. *Teaching and Learning English as a Foreign Language.* Ann Arbor: Univ. Mich. Press, 1945. (Chapter 2 describes the phonemic system used in the materials of the English Language Institute of the University of Michigan.)

--------. *The Structure of English: An Introduction to the Construction of English Sentences.* New York: Harcourt, Brace and Company, 1952, ix, 304 pp. (Based on a linguistic analysis of recorded conversations totaling more than 250,000 words.)

--------, and Traver, A. Aileen. *English Word Lists: A Study of Their Adaptability for Instruction* (prepared for the Committee on Modern Languages of the American Council on Education). Washington, D. C.: American Council on Education, 1940. Ann Arbor: The George Wahr Publishing Co., reprinted 1950. ix, 109 pp. (A critical analysis of vocabulary lists; not a list of words.)

Galinsky, Hans. *Die Sprache des Amerikaners: Eine Einführung*

*in die Hauptunterschiede zwischen amerikanischem und briti-
schem Englisch der Gegenwart.* Vol I. Heidelberg: Kerle, 1951.
vii, 217 pp. (Discusses differences in pronunciation, intonation,
and stress between American and British English. Reviewed
by Herbert Penzl in *American Speech,* 28 (1952): 39-42.)

Haugen, Einar. "The Learning of English," Chapter 3 of *The
Norwegian Language in America,* Vol. I. Philadelphia: Univ.
Penn. Press, 1953.

Hayden, Rebecca. "The Relative Frequency of Phonemes in
General-American English," *Word,* 6, No. 3 (1950), 217-23.

Jespersen, Otto. *A Modern English Grammar on Historical
Principles.* Heidelberg: Carl Winter's Universitätsbuchhand-
lung. Part I (3d ed.) 1922, xi, 485 pp.; Part II (2d ed.) 1922,
xxviii, 486 pp.; Part III, 1927, ix, 415 pp.; Part IV, 1931, xxxi,
400 pp. (Based on thousands of examples collected from English literature.)

---------. *Essentials of English Grammar.* New York: Henry
Holt and Company, 1933, 1939. 287 pp. (Based on quotations
from English prose.)

Jones, Daniel. *An English Pronouncing Dictionary, Containing
56,280 Words in International Phonetic Transcription* (7th ed.,
rev., with supplement). New York: E. P. Dutton and Company,
Inc., 1946, xxviii, 490 pp., diagrams. (The pronunciation rep-
presented is that of educated people in the South of England —
Received Standard. For a dictionary of American pronunciation see Kenyon and Knott.)

---------. *An Outline of English Phonetics* (7th ed.). Cambridge,
Eng.: W. Heffer and Sons Ltd., 1950, x, 328 pp., illustrated.
(Describes British English with reference to a system of
"cardinal vowels." Uses the Armstrong and Ward system of
dots and short curves to represent intonation.)

Jones, Lawrence G. "The Vowels of English and Russian: An
Acoustic Comparison," *Word,* 9 (1953), 354-61.

Kennedy, Arthur G. *A Bibliography of Writings on the English
Language from the Beginning of Printing to the End of 1922.*
Cambridge and New Haven: Harvard Univ. Press, Yale Univ.
Press, 1927, xvii, 517 pp. (For the years since 1922 see the
Annual Bibliography of English Language and Literature,
published by Bowes and Bowes, 1920-1934, Cambridge Univer-
sity Press, 1935-present, and the bibliographies in *American
Speech.*)

--------. *A Concise Bibliography for Students of English; Systematically Arranged* (2d ed.). Stanford: Stanford Univ. Press, 1945, vii, 161 pp.

Kenyon, John S. *American Pronunciation* (9th ed.). Ann Arbor: George Wahr Publishing Co., 1946, ix, 248 pp.

Kenyon, John S., and Knott, Thomas A. *A Pronouncing Dictionary of American English*. Springfield, Mass.: G. and C. Merriam Company, 1944, lii, 484 pp. (Standard colloquial American English in slightly modified I. P. A. notation. Some regional variations also recorded.)

Kruisinga, E., and Erades, P. A. *An English Grammar*. Vol. I, *Accidence and Syntax* (7th ed.). Groningen, Netherlands: P. Noordhoff N. V. First Part, 1947, 1-277 pp; Second Part, 1950, 279-606 pp. (Based on contemporary literary English usage.)

Kurath, Hans. *A Word Geography of the Eastern United States* (Studies American English, Number 1). Ann Arbor: Univ. Mich. Press, 1949, xi, 88 pp., with 164 full-page maps.

Lado, Robert. *Annotated Bibliography for Teachers of English as a Foreign Language* (Bulletin 1955, No. 3, U. S. Dept. Health, Education, and Welfare: Office of Education). Washington, D. C.: Government Printing Office, 1955, vii, 224 pp.

Lindblom, Eila Maria. "On Finnish Consonant Phonemes and their Comparison with Corresponding English Phonemes," *Language Learning,* 5, Nos. 3 and 4 (1955), 88-93.

Lorge, Irving. *The Semantic Count of the 570 Commonest English Words*. New York: Bureau of Publications, Teachers College, Columbia University, 1949, xiii, 187 pp. (Gives frequency rating for each meaning of a word as defined in the *Oxford English Dictionary,* Vols. I-XII and Supplement. Supplements Irving Lorge and Edward L. Thorndike, "A Semantic Count of English Words." New York: The Institute of Educational Research, Teachers College, Columbia University, 1938. (Unpublished). Results used in West, Michael, *A General Service List of English Words*.)

Marckwardt, Albert H., and Walcott, Fred G. *Facts About Current English Usage, Including a Discussion of Current Usage in Grammar from 'Current English Usage' by S. A. Leonard* (A Publication of the National Council of Teachers of English). New York and London: D. Appleton-Century Company, 1938, viii, 144 pp.

McIntosh, Lois. "A Description and Comparison of Question Signals in Spoken English, Mandarin Chinese, French and German for Teachers of English as a Foreign Language." Doctoral Dissertation, University of Michigan (Microfilmed). vii, 238 pp.

Modern Humanities Research Association. *Annual Bibliography of English Language and Literature*. Bowes and Bowes, 1920-1934, Cambridge University Press, 1935 to date.

Nasr, Raja T. "The Phonological Problems Involved in Teaching of American English to Native Speakers of Lebanese Arabic." Doctoral Dissertation, University of Michigan (Microfilmed).

Newman, Stanley S. "On the Stress System of English," *Word*, 2, No. 3 (1946), 171-87.

Ogden, C. K. *The Basic Words, a Detailed Account of Their Uses*. London: Psyche Miniatures, 1933.

Pike, Kenneth L. "On the Phonemic Status of English Diphthongs," *Language*, 23 (1947), 151-59.

--------. *Phonemics: A Technique for Reducing Languages to Writing*. Ann Arbor: Univ. Mich. Press, 1947. (Pages 44-53 contain essentially the phonemic analysis used in the materials of the English Language Institute of the University of Michigan. Description and footnotes refer to the different interpretations and notation of several American linguists. The nonnative speaker of English might find it necessary to refer to the textbook *English Pronunciation: Exercises in Sound Segments, Intonation, and Rhythm,* by the Research Staff of the English Language Institute, Charles C. Fries, Director, to understand the sound system described.)

--------. *The Intonation of American English*. Ann Arbor: Univ. Mich. Press, 1945, xi, 199 pp.

Piroch, Goldie. "The Importance of Bilingual Description to Foreign Language Learning," *Language Learning*, 6, Nos. 1 and 2 (1955), 51-61. (Pronunciation problems of Slovac speakers learning English.)

Quizon Santos, Maria. "Simple Questions with *Be* for Pampango Speakers," *Language Learning*, 5, Nos. 1 and 2 (1953-54), 61-63.

Reed, David W., Lado, Robert, and Shen, Yao. "The Importance of the Native Language in Foreign Language Learning,"

Language Learning, 1, No. 1 (1948), 17-23. (Pronunciation problems of Spanish, Chinese, and Portuguese speakers learning English.)

Rinsland, Henry D. *A Basic Vocabulary of Elementary School Children*. New York: The Macmillan Company, 1945, 636 pp.

Rostzke, H. A. "Vowel-Length in General American Speech," *Language*, 15, 99-109.

Schwab, William. "Some Structural Problems for Tagalog Students in English," *Language Learning*, 6, Nos. 1 and 2 (1955), 68-72.

Seashore, Robert H. "How Many Words do Children Know?" *The Packet: Heath's Service Bulletin for Elementary Teachers*, 2, No. 2 (1947), 3-17. Boston: D. C. Heath and Company. (Reports much larger vocabularies than previously estimated. From 1,900 basic words for Grade 1 to 46,500 for Grade 12, and from 24,000 to 80,000 basic and derived words for the same grades.)

Shen, Yao. "Two English Modification Patterns for Chinese Students," *Language Learning*, 1, No. 4 (1948), 19-22.

Simley, Anne. "A Study of Norwegian Dialect in Minnesota," *American Speech*, 5 (1930), 469-74.

Sitachitta, Kanda. "A Brief Comparison of English and Thai Questions," *Language Learning*, 5, Nos. 3 and 4 (1955), 130-34.

Swadesh, Morris. "On the Analysis of English Syllabics," *Language*, 23 (1947), 137-51.

Thomas, Charles K. *An Introduction to the Phonetics of American English*. New York: The Ronald Press Co., 1947. ix, 181 pp.

Thorndike, Edward L., and Lorge, Irving. *The Teacher's Word Book of 30,000 Words*. New York: Bureau of Publications, Teachers College Columbia University, 1944, 274 pp.

Trager, George L., and Bloch, Bernard. "The Syllabic Phonemes of English," *Language*, 17, No. 3 (1941), 223-46.

Trager, George L., and Smith, Henry Lee, Jr. *An Outline of English Structure*. (Studies in Linguistics: Occasional Papers, No. 3.) Norman, Okla.: Battenberg Press, 1951. 92 pp. (For an adaptation of the phonemic analysis described see *Structural Notes and Corpus; A Basis for the Preparation of*

Materials to Teach English as a Foreign Language. Published
by the Committee on the Language Program, American Council of Learned Societies, Washington, D. C., 1952. For explanations to teachers using the *Spoken English Textbooks,*
ACLS Program in English as a Foreign Language, see Wel-
mers, William E., *Spoken English as a Foreign Language;
Instructors Manual.* Washington, D. C.: American Council of
Learned Societies, 1953, 27 pp.)

Wallace, Betty Jane. "A Quantitative Analysis of Consonant
Clusters in Present-Day English." Doctoral Dissertation,
University of Michigan. (Microfilmed: *Microfilm Abstracts,*
11 (1951), 336-37.)

Ward, Ida C. *The Phonetics of English* (4th ed., reprinted 1952).
Cambridge, Eng.: W. Heffer and Sons, Ltd., xv, 255 pp., illustrated.

West, Michael. *A General Service List of English Words, with
Semantic Frequencies and a Supplementary Word-List for the
Writing of Popular Science and Technology.* London, New
York, Toronto: Longmans, Green, and Co., 1953, xiii, 588 pp.

Wolff, Hans. "Partial Comparison of the Sound System of English
and Puerto-Rican Spanish," *Language Learning,* 3, Nos. 1 and
2 (1950), 38-40.

FINNISH

Sauvageot, Aurélien. *Esquisse de la langue finnoise.* In Les
langues et leurs structures I. Paris: C. Klincksieck, 1949,
250 pp.

FRENCH

Cheydleur, Frederic D. *French Idiom List, Based on a Running
Count of 1,183,000 Words* (Publications of the American and
Canadian Committees on Modern Languages, Vol. XVI). New
York, 1929.

Coutenoble, H. N. *Studies in French Intonation.* Cambridge,
Eng.: W. Heffer & Sons Ltd., 1934, xvi, 278 pp.

Genevrier, P. *Précis de phonétique comparée française et
anglaise.* Paris: H. Didier, 1927. 372 pp.

Hall, Robert A., Jr. *French*. (Language Monograph No. 24. Structural Sketches 1.) Supplement to *Language*, 24, No. 3, 1948, 56 pp.

Henmon, V. A. C. *A French Word Book Based on a Count of 400,000 Running Words*. Madison: Bureau of Educational Research Bulletin, No. 3, University of Wisconsin, 1924.

Martinet, André. *La pronunciation du Français contemporain: témoignages recueillis en 1941 dans un camp d'officiers prisonniers*. (Société de Publications Romanes et Françaises, No. 23.) Paris: Librairie E. Droz, 1945, 249 pp.

Seward, Robert D. *Dictionary of French Cognates*. New York: S. F. Vanni.

Vander Beke, George E. *French Word Book*. New York: The Macmillan Company, 1939, 188 pp.

GERMAN

Hauch, Edward F. *A German Idiom List, Selected on the Basis of Frequency and Range of Occurrence*. Publications of the American and Canadian Committees on Modern Languages, Vol. X. New York, 1929.

Morgan, B. Q. *A German Frequency Word Book, Based on Kaeding's Häufigkeitswörterbuch der deutschen Sprache*. Publications of the American and Canadian Committees on Modern Languages, Vol. IX, New York, 1928.

HUNGARIAN

Hall, Robert A., Jr. *Hungarian Grammar*. (Language Monograph No. 21.) Baltimore: Linguistic Society of America, 1944.

Lotz, J. *Das ungarische Sprachsystem*. Budapest, 1939. Reviewed in *Language*, 19 (1943), 55-58.

ITALIAN

Hall, Robert A., Jr. *Bibliography of Italian Linguistics*. Baltimore: Linguistic Society of America, 1941, 543 pp.

————. *Descriptive Italian Grammar*. Ithaca: Cornell Univ. Press and Linguistic Society of America, 1948, xi, 228 pp.

137

JAPANESE

Bloch, Bernard. "Studies in Colloquial Japanese." Part I, "Inflection," *Journal of American Oriental Society,* 66 (1946), 97-109; Part II, "Syntax," *Language,* 22 (1946), 200-248; Part III, "Derivation of Inflected Words," *Journal of American Oriental Society,* 66 (1946), 304-15; Part IV, "Phonemics," *Language,* 26 (1950), 86-125.

Jorden, Eleanor Harz. *The Syntax of Modern Colloquial Japanese.* (Language Dissertation No. 52.) Supplement to *Language,* 31, No. 1 (Part 3), 1955. Baltimore: Linguistic Society of America. v, 135 pp.

Martin, Samuel E. *Morphophonemics of Standard Colloquial Japanese.* (Language Dissertation No. 47). Supplement to *Language,* 28, No. 3 (Part 2), 1952. Baltimore: Linguistic Society of America, 115 pp.

KOREAN

Martin, Samuel. "Korean Phonemics," *Language,* 27 (1951), 519-33.

--------. *Korean Morphophonemics.* Special Publications of the Linguistic Society of America, 1954.

NORWEGIAN

Haugen, Einar. *The Norwegian Language in America: A Study in Bilingual Behavior.* Vol. I, The Bilingual Community, xiv, 317 pp; Vol. II, The American Dialects of Norwegian, vii, 377 pp. Philadelphia: Univ. Penn. Press, 1953.

PERSIAN

Lucidi, Mario. "L'accento nel persiano moderno," *Studi Linguistiche,* 2 (1951), 108-40.

PHILIPPINE LANGUAGES

Bloomfield, Leonard. "Outline of Ilocano Syntax," *Language,* 18, No. 3 (1942), 193-200.

Bloomfield, Leonard. *Tagalog Texts with Grammatical Analysis*. (University of Illinois studies in language and literature. Vol. III, No. 2-4) Urbana: University of Illinois, 1917.

PORTUGUESE

Allen, Joseph H. D., Jr. *Portuguese Word-Formation with Suffixes*. (Language Dissertation No. 33.) Baltimore: Linguistic Society of America, 1941, 143 pp.

Brown, Charles B., and others. *A Graded Word Book of Brazilian Portuguese*. New York: F. S. Crofts & Co., 1945. 252 pp.

Hall, Robert A., Jr. "The Unit Phonemes of Brazilian Portuguese," *Studies in Linguistics*, 1, No. 15 (1943).

Pap, L. *Portuguese-American Speech: An Outline of Speech Conditions among Portuguese Immigrants in New England and Elsewhere in the United States*. New York: King's Crown Press, 1949, xi, 223 pp.

Reed, David W., and Leite, Yolanda. "The Segmental Phonemes of Brazilian Portuguese: Standard Paulista Dialect." In *Phonemics* by Kenneth L. Pike (Ann Arbor: Univ. Mich. Press, 1947), pp. 194-202.

RUMANIAN

Rosetti, A. *Grammaire de la langue roumaine*. Bucharest, 1944, 216 pp.

RUSSIAN

Josselson, Harry H. *The Russian Word Count and Frequency Analysis of Grammatical Categories of Standard Literary Russian*. Detroit: Wayne Univ. Press, 1953, 274 pp.

Unbegaun, B. O., with the collaboration of J. C. G. Simmons. *A Bibliographical Guide to the Russian Language*. Oxford: Clarendon Press, 1953, xi, 174 pp. (See review by Roman Jacobson in *Word*, 9 (1953), 400-407, for important additions.)

SPANISH

Alarcos Llorach, Emilio. *Fonología española (según el método de la Escuela de Praga)*. Madrid: Gredos, 1950. 160 pp.

--------. *Gramática estructural (según la escuela de Copenhague y con especial atención a la lengua española)*. Madrid: Editorial Gredos, 1951. 129 pp.

Alonso, Amado, y Henríquez Ureña, Pedro. *Gramática castellana* (3d ed.). Buenos Aires: Editorial Losada, 1943. Primer curso, 238 pp. Segundo curso, 239 pp.

Anthony, Ann. "A Structural Approach to the Analysis of Spanish Intonation," *Language Learning*, 1, No. 3 (1948), 24-31.

Bello, Andrés. *Gramática de la langua castellana* (23d ed., with notes by D. Rufino José Cuervo). Paris: Andrés Blot, editor, 1928. 366 pp. + 160 (Notas) pp.

Bowen, J. Donald. "A Comparison of the Intonation Patterns of English and Spanish," *Hispania*, 39, No. 1 (March, 1956), 30-35.

Buchanan, Milton A. *A Graded Spanish Word Book*. (Publications of the American and Canadian Committee on Modern Languages, Vol. III.) Toronto: Toronto Univ. Press, 1941. 195 pp.

Entrambasaguas, Joaquín de. *Síntesis de pronunciación española*. Madrid: Consejo Superior de Investigaciones Científicas, 1952, 156 pp.

Keniston, Hayward. *A Basic List of Spanish Words and Idioms*. Chicago: Univ. Chi. Press, 1933.

--------. *A Spanish Idiom List, Selected on the Basis of Range and Frequency of Occurrence*. Publications of the American and Canadian Committees on Modern Languages, Vol. XI, New York, 1937.

--------. *Spanish Syntax List*. (Publications of the Committee on Modern Languages.) New York: Henry Holt and Company, 1937, 278 pp.

Lado, Robert. "A Comparison of the Sound Systems of English and Spanish," *Hispania*, 39, No. 1 (March, 1956), 26-29.

Lenz, Rodolfo. *La oración y sus partes* (3d. ed.). Madrid: Tip. y Enc. de Senén Martín, 1935, 571 pp.

Navarro Tomás, Tomás. *Manual de entonación española* (2d. ed). New York: Hispanic Institute, 1948. 306 pp. (With four phonograph records.)

––––––––. *Manual de pronunciación española* (4th ed., revised, corrected, and enlarged). Madrid: Publicaciones de la *Revista de filología española,* 1932.

Nunn, Marshall E., and Van Scroy, Herbert A. *Glossary of Related Spanish-English Words.* University, Ala.: Univ. Ala. Studies, Number 5, 1949, 68 pp.

Real Academia Española. *Diccionario de la lengua española.* Madrid: Espasa-Calpe, S. A., 1936, 1334 pp.

––––––––. *Gramática de la lengua española* (new corrected ed.). Madrid: Espasa-Calpe, S. A., 1931, 534 pp.

Rodríguez Bou, Ismael, director. *Recuento de vocabulario español.* Río Piedras, Puerto Rico: University of Puerto Rico, 1952. Vol. I, xix, 668 pp. Vol. II, Part I, xv, 566 pp; Part II, x, 567-1090 pp.

Saporta, Sol. "Problems in the Comparison of the Morphemic Systems of English and Spanish," *Hispania,* 39, No. 1 (March, 1956); 36-40.

TAMIL

Fowler, Murray. "The Segmental Phonemes of Sanskritized Tamil," *Language,* 30, 360-67.

THAI

Fowler, Murray, and Israsena, Tasniya. *The Total Distribution of the Sounds of Siamese.* Madison: Univ. Wis. Press, 1952

VIETNAMESE

Emeneau, M. B. *Studies in Vietnamese (Annamese) Grammar.* Berkeley and Los Angeles: Univ. Calif. Press, 1954, x, 235 pp.

YIDDISH

Weinreich, Uriel. *College Yiddish, An Introduction to the Yiddish Language and to Jewish Life and Culture*. New York: Yiddish Scientific Institute, 1949. 397 pp.

--------. "Stress and Word Structure in Yiddish," *The Field of Yiddish: Studies in Language, Folklore, and Literature* (ed. Uriel Weinreich). New York: Linguistic Circle of New York, Columbia University, 1954. Pp. 1-27.